THE
JUICE
2008

The Juice
by Matt Skinner

First published in Great Britain in 2007 by Mitchell Beazley, an imprint of Octopus Publishing Group Limited, 2–4 Heron Quays, London E14 4JP.

ISBN 978 1 84533 335 5

A CIP catalogue record for this book is available from the British Library.

Set in Helvetica
Colour reproduction by Graphic Studio in Italy
Printed and bound by Toppan in China

The author and publishers will be grateful for any information which will assist them in keeping future editions up-to-date. Although all reasonable care has been taken in the preparation of this book, neither the publishers nor the author can accept any liability for any consequences arising from the use thereof, or the information contained therein.

Commissioning Editor: Rebecca Spry
Concept Design: Matt Utber
Layout Design: Yasia Williams-Leedham
Managing Editor: Hilary Azzam
Editor: Jamie Ambrose; Philippa Bell
Photographs by Chris Terry
Production: Peter Hunt

The Juice Team and Mitchell Beazley would like to thank the following for their help in sourcing bottle images:
ABS Wine Agencies, Armit Wines, Bell Hill Vineyard, Berkmann Wines, Berry Bros & Rudd, Bibendum Wines, Bonny Doon Vineyard, Bordeaux Index, Brown Brothers Milawa, Codorniu, Constellation Wines, Craggy Range, De Bortoli UK, Diamond Creek Vineyards, Fells, Fields Morris & Verdin, Fine Wine Partners, Fosters Australia, Gaja Winery, Genesis Wines, Great Western Wine, Hailsham Cellars, Hallgarten Wines, Hatch Mansfield, HwCg, Innocent Bystander, Kangarilla Road, Katnook Estate, Kracher, Lea & Sandeman, Leeuwin Estate, Liberty Wines, Margan Family Winegrowers, MMD, Negociants UK, Nepenthe Wines, Planeta, Limm Communications, Poliziano, Rathbone Wine Group, Ridgeview Wine Estate, Rustenberg Wines, Tanners Wine Merchants, Waitrose, Wine & Partners, Yering Station.

Contents

The Juice 2008: 100 wines you should be drinking

For three years now I've put together this book within easy reach of home, work, and play, and to be honest, it would've been just as easy to do the same again this year. But experience tells me comfort zones can be horrible things, and so I decided to run away to Barcelona for a few days in search of some inspiration.

For 48 blissful hours my team and I ate, drank, wandered, made some new friends, laughed, observed, slept a little, and then ate and drank some more. I've included the photos from this trip because I wanted you to see one of my favourite food and wine cultures in action. This is a culture where food and wine are celebrated on a daily basis; a culture where there is little room for pretension; a culture where, most importantly, people of all ages regularly come together to eat and drink.

Over the coming year, step outside your comfort zone wherever possible. Once a week, spend a little bit more on your wine, bearing in mind that trading up doesn't have to mean shelling out. Try something new: new varieties, new styles, new producers, and new frontiers. Often that's where you'll find some of the most exciting wines, not to mention the best value.

Pay more attention to what you eat – it's a great way to learn about food-and-wine matching. Visit a vineyard, ask lots of questions, do a wine course with a friend, run away to Barcelona for a few days – but most importantly, resolve to finish the coming year knowing a little bit more about wine than you did 12 months earlier.

Más Amor,

How It All Works

What began life as a weekly email sent out to friends and workmates in a vain attempt to help them drink better has now become a regular distillation of our drinking year. As with previous editions, *The Juice 2008* combines 100 wine recommendations, together with a few handy tips and little bits of wisdom. Think of it as the big kid's survival guide to Planet Wine – or better still, a huge step toward better drinking.

So here's the drill. I thought that rather than ranking the wines one to 100, it'd be far more useful if I grouped the wines by occasion. And so, as with previous years, I've split our 100 wines into five easy groups of 20 wines each: DRINK, GIVE, DINE, SPLURGE, and STASH. There's something here for everyone – every taste, every budget, and for every occasion.

Wherever possible I've tried to review the most current vintage; in some cases this means wines that are only just hitting the streets now. And while some might not be gracing the shelves of your local just yet (frustrating as that may be), be patient: they will come!

Listed stockists are a mix of supermarkets, national chains, smaller independent wine retailers and online wine merchants. The idea is that you should be able to get your hands on many of the 100 wines without too much heartache.

Happy Drinking!

The Juice Awards

Having to pick specifics from my list
of 100 wines is the least enjoyable part
of this project, and if at all possible –
and much to the annoyance of my
editor – I try and dodge the job for as
long as I can. They're all good for one
reason or another, and in my opinion
putting a select few on a pedestal is
largely an academic exercise. Still, it's
true that there are always a couple that
stand out for one reason or another,
and so without any further ado, here
are the wines that in 2007 pushed
our collective buttons.

WINE OF THE YEAR

Punica Barrua 2004
Sardinia, Italy

The most exciting thing about the world of wine is watching stars rise, new producers, re-emerging regions, and old varieties – rarely, if ever, is there a dull moment. Few would disagree that the ongoing rise of Italy's southern half has been a hot topic. Campania, Puglia, Sicily, and Sardinia have produced a dizzying range of wines – both in terms of quality and price. In my opinion not only is Punica Barrua 2004 from Sardinia exceptional, but it manages to effortlessly tick all the right boxes. Hunt it down.

BARGAIN OF THE YEAR

Willunga 100 Grenache 2005
McLaren Vale, Australia

Competition for this award has never been hotter. The world is awash with any number of keenly priced, ready-to-drink gems. This year Bargain of the Year goes to a wine that has blown onto the scene and dropped jaws aplenty with its sheer level of fruit, its immediate wow factor, its depth, balance, and purity. You would happily pay two, possibly three times the money for this wine, but, as it stands, this year's winner – Willunga 100 Grenache 2005 – will set you back a mere £7.99. So, what are you waiting for? Fill your house with it.

PRODUCER OF THE YEAR

Peter Lehmann Wines
Barossa Valley, Australia

There's no doubt that being a wine producer in this day and age is far from easy. Global overproduction and an environment in crisis – you'd have to have rocks in your head. Still, there are plenty who continue to smile and, despite the odds, consistently produce stunning wines for all the right reasons. This year, although there were many contenders, there was one producer whose name continued to pop up. From the knockout entry-level all the way through to the polished company flagship, "Stonewell", Peter Lehmann produce a range of wines that rarely, if ever, fails to impress.

The Varieties

Wine comes in all different shapes and sizes: big wines, little wines, fat wines, skinny wines, good wines, great wines, wines that absolutely blow your mind. And while what happens in the winery plays a big role in determining how a wine might end up, each variety has its own distinctive personality – personality you can *taste*.

With the number of grape varieties on the planet running into the thousands, what follows is a brief run-down of the most popular that you're likely to encounter – plus a few extra that popped up in this year's *Juice*.

THE WHITES

Albariño (*al-bah-RIN-yo*)

Albariño (Alvariñho in Portugal) is native to Spain's Galicia region where it produces the knock-out dry whites of Rías Baixas. It's also an important blending tool in Portugal's *vinho verde*, where it sports lighter personality. The character of great Albariño lies somewhere between Riesling and Viognier, often displaying plenty of ripe citrus zip and zing coupled with apricot, flowers, and sweet spice. Weight means Albariño can handle some oak, although it's not often employed.

Chardonnay (*SHAR-do-nay*)

Love it or loathe it, you can't deny this grape its place in wine's hall of fame. Some of the very best examples hail from Burgundy, where texture, finesse, structure, and ageing ability rule over simple "drink-now" fruit flavours. You see, Chardonnay comes in all different shapes and sizes. Flavours range from the delicate, citrus, and slightly honeyed styles of Chablis to warmer, Southern-hemisphere styles, where aromas range from peaches and pears to full-throttle, ripe, tropical fruits like banana, pineapple, guava, and mango.

Chenin Blanc (*shuh-NIN BLAHN*)

Handier than a Swiss army knife, the globetrotting Chenin's high natural acidity and tendency to flirt with botrytis lend it equally well to a variety of styles; sweet, dry, and fizzy. A good traveller, Chenin's stomping ground is France's Loire Valley, where it makes racy dry whites, luscious sweet wines, and clean, frothy fizz. Expect aromas of apples, gooseberries, and fresh herbs.

Gewürztraminer (*geh-VERZ-trah-MEE-ner*)

Like a drag queen with too much make-up and perfume (and little shame), this is the incredibly camp member of the white-grape family. In reality, Gewürz is one of the superstar varieties of Alsace in France. The best ooze aromas of lychee, rose, orange blossom, cinnamon, ginger, and spice. Good Gewürz will be rich and weighty, with great length of flavour.

Grüner Veltliner (*GREW-ner velt-LEE-ner*)

If you haven't heard of Grüner Veltliner, where have you been?! The *über*-cool variety of Austria is often likened to Chardonnay for its weight and intensity, but it's spicier, with smells of miso paste, ginger, and wet wool.

Marsanne

Clean, fresh, fruity, this grape plays second fiddle to Viognier in France's northern Rhône Valley; however, it dominates many of the white-wine blends of the southern Rhône. Expect ripe, peachy fruit flavours, fresh acidity, and barely a whiff of oak. With a bit of age, Marsanne takes on an amazing honeyed character and becomes slightly oilier, with more weight and richness. Outside France, you might see it in parts of Australia.

Muscat

For purposes of this book, the large Muscat family of grapes can be split into non-identical triplets: Muscat Blanc à Petits Grains, Muscat of Alexandria, and Muscat Ottonel. Wine styles vary from light, fizzy

Moscato d'Asti (northwest Italy) and sweet, spirity Muscat de Beaumes-de-Venise (France's Rhône Valley) to Spain's aromatic Málagas and the unique liqueur Muscats of Australia's northeast Victoria.

Palomino Fino
(pal-o-MEEN-o FEEN-o)
The most important variety in the production of sherry, accounting for four of the five main styles: manzanilla, fino, amontillado, and oloroso. Fino's the most popular and one of the greatest food wines in the world. The best are bone-dry, nutty, and slightly salty, with great mineral texture and a clean, tangy finish.

Pedro Ximénez
(PAY-dro hee-MAY-neth)
Although "PX", as it's more commonly called, falls into the white-grape family, this sun-loving variety produces sweet, thick, syrupy wines. Great examples are almost black in colour, viscous, and super-sweet, with intense aromas of raisin and spice.

Pinot Gris/Pinot Grigio
(PEE-no gree/PEE-no GREE-jee-o)
Technically, these are the same grape; the key difference lies in the style. Pinot Grigio tends to be light, delicate, and fresh, usually made in stainless-steel tanks and best drunk young, when it's zippy and vibrant. Pinot Gris is fatter and richer, with more weight and intensity, often from time spent in oak. Pinot Grigio is commonly found in the cool of northeast Italy, while Pinot Gris is never more at home than in the French region of Alsace.

Riesling *(REES-ling)*
Technically brilliant but still a wee bit nerdy, Riesling currently represents some of this planet's great bargain wine buys. While its spiritual home is Germany, you'll find world-class examples from Austria, France, and Australia. The best will have beautiful, pure, citrus-fruit aromas alongside fresh-cut flowers and spice, with flavours of lemons, limes, and minerals.

Sauvignon Blanc
(SO-vin-yon BLAHN)

Think passion-fruit, gooseberry, elderflower, blackcurrant … even cat's pee (really!). France, South Africa, Chile, and Australia all have a good crack at it, but New Zealand (Marlborough, to be exact) is the modern home of this variety. The best examples are pale, unmistakably pungent on the nose, painfully crisp, and ultra-refreshing with plenty of zip and racy acidity.

Sémillon (SEM-ee-yon)

Sémillon is native to Bordeaux in France, but it's Down Under in New South Wales's Hunter Valley where Semillon (no é here) has had greatest success, producing beautifully crafted and insanely long-lived wines. In its youth, great examples explode with pear, white peach, and other ripe summer fruits. But stash a bottle away for a rainy day a few years down the line, and you'll witness this variety's true magic:

aromas of super-intense citrus fruit, even marmalade, alongside toast, honey, nuts, and sweet spice.

Verdicchio (vehr-DIK-ee-o)

Verdicchio is grown and produced in Italy's Marche region, making big, rich whites that are pretty neutral when it comes to aroma, but super-lemony in flavour with plenty of spice and richness. Because of its weight, it can handle oak, too, so expect to see some wooded examples.

Viognier (vee-ON-yay)

Viognier overflows with intoxicating aromas of apricots, orange rind, and fresh-cut flowers. It's weighty, rich, and oily in texture, with great length and beautifully soft acidity. Native to France's northern Rhône, it also shows promise in Australia and South Africa.

THE REDS

Cabernet Sauvignon
(KAB-er-nay SO-veen-yon)
King of the red grapes, the best display power, finesse, elegance, the ability to age, and universal appeal. Its home was Bordeaux, but particularly good examples now also come from Italy, Spain, Chile, Argentina, South Africa, Australia, and California. The range of flavours and aromas varies greatly, but look for blackcurrant, dark cherry, and plummy fruit alongside cedar, mint, and eucalyptus.

Carignan *(CAHR-een-yahn)*
The sun-lovin' Carignan makes full-bodied, slightly rustic, tannic reds. Once among the most widely planted red grapes on the planet, many Carignan vineyards have since been yanked out to make way for more fashionable (and reliable) Syrah and Grenache. The best come from old vines, and Languedoc-Roussillon in the south of France has some of the oldest. Carignan also pops up in the USA, Spain, and Italy.

Carmenère *(car-meh-NAIR)*
Carmenère can be a nightmare in the vineyard: it's hard to get ripe, and once it is, you have a tiny window in which to pick it before the acidity disappears. But when it's good, it's really good! Bearing an uncanny likeness to Merlot, the best examples are bursting with super-dark fruits (plums, blackberries, and black cherries) and aromas of spice and leather.

Grenache *(GRIN-ash)*
Grown widely in Spain, France, and Australia, Grenache is the workhorse of red grapes, and can be a stand-alone performer in its own right. As concentrated, weighty, fully fledged reds (especially in France's southern Rhône), the wines sit comfortably alongside some of the world's greatest. It also provides the base for many rosés: its tannin, acidity, and good whack of alcohol go perfect in pink.

Malbec

This red grape variety loves the sun and is found in Argentina's Andes Mountains (home to a handful of the highest-altitude vineyards on earth). These are big wines, and the best are soft and super-fruity, with plums and spice.

Merlot (*MER-low*)

Merlot has long played second fiddle to Big Brother Cabernet, often sidelined for blending. Yet it's the most widely planted red grape in Bordeaux, and in recent times, both California and Australia have developed a love affair with it. New World examples tend to be plump, with ripe, plummy fruit and naturally low tannin. Wines from north of the equator are drier, leaner, and generally less in-your-face.

Mourvèdre (*moor-VED-rah*)

The star of the southern Rhône. Along with dark, sweet fruit there's mushroom, tobacco, roast lamb – even the elephant pen at the zoo! In Spain, it's known as Monastrell and Mataro, while in Australia it goes by Mataro and Mourvèdre. Because of its funkiness, it's rarely produced as a solo variety and is usually reserved for blending.

Nebbiolo (*neb-ee-YO-lo*)

The best examples are layered and complex, oozing aromas of tar, roses, dark cherry, black olives, and rosemary. In great wines, concentrated fruit, firm acidity, and a wash of drying tannins ensure that they'll go the distance if you want to stash them away. Nebbiolo's home is Piedmont, where it stacks up to everything, from mushrooms (truffles) to chicken, rabbit, and all sorts of game right through to old, mouldy cheeses.

Nero d'Avola (*NEHR-o DAV-o-lah*)

A red star of southern Italy, especially Sicily. These wines pack masses of fruit – dark plum, morello cherry – along with Mediterranean spice and earth. The best of these wines benefit from a stint in the cellar, but much is now made into well-priced wines with immediate appeal.

Pinot Noir (*PEE-no NWAR*)
Top examples of Pinot are seductive, intriguing, even sexy, and their versatility with food is near unrivalled. Thought of as one of the lightest reds, top examples show layers of strawberry, raspberry, plum, and dark forest fruits, with aromas of earth, spice, animal, cedar, and truffle. These wines range from delicate and minerally to silky and rich. Try those from the Côte de Nuits (Burgundy), and New Zealand's Central Otago and Martinborough regions.

Primitivo/Zinfandel
For ages we thought these were different varieties, but they're actually the same. Zinfandel ("Zin" for short) is found in the mighty USA, where most things big are seen as beautiful. In southern Italy, Primitivo rides high alongside Negroamaro and Nero d'Avola. With plenty of sweet, ripe fruit and aromas of violets and leather, this style is much more restrained than its transatlantic brother.

Sangiovese (*san-gee-o-VAY-zay*)
Loaded with aromas of dark cherry, plum, and forest fruits, Sangiovese often also smells of tobacco, spice, and earth. Most remember its trademark "super-drying" tannins, which, without food, can make this grape a hard slog. It's native to Tuscany, where it shines as Chianti Classico and Brunello di Montalcino. More recently, it has surfaced in both Australia and the USA, but so far without the same success.

Syrah/Shiraz (*SIH-rah/SHEER-az*)
Syrah is the French name for this grape. Lighter in body than Shiraz, with aromas of redcurrants, raspberry, plum, and nearly always white pepper and spice. Shiraz ends to be concentrated and ripe. At its best, it oozes plum, raspberry, earth, cedar, and freshly ground pepper. Some New World winemakers are now calling their

wines Syrah to reflect the difference in style from Shiraz.

Tempranillo (*tem-pra-NEE-yo*)

The grand old man of Spanish wine. Native to Rioja, it has also sunk its roots in nearby Ribera del Duero, Navarra, Priorato, and Toro. Typically, it has a solid core of dark berry fruits complete with a rustic edge that relies on savoury aromas such as tobacco, spice, leather, and earth. A recent trend has been to make international styles with big colour, big fruit, and big oak.

Touriga Nacional (*too-REE-ga nas-see-o-NAHL*)

Touriga plays a starring role in many of Portugal's great fortified wines as well as being an important component in more than a few of its new-wave table wines. Deep, densely fruited, leathery, and with an almost inky texture, Touriga needs time to mellow. Expect to smell things like dried fruit, leather, and violets, while fortified wines will be richer, stacked with dried-fruit flavour, and boasting plenty of sweetness.

The Hot 100

Drink

Give

Dine

Splurge

Stash

Partying, food, getting around, rent, bills, and roughly in that order… there are a million-and-one ways to spend your hard-earned cash. The reality is that for most of us, a decent bottle of wine just isn't up at the sharp end of the list. Which is why, in this chapter, we lift the lid on the best wines for the least money. So no more excuses: what could you go without this month in order to drink better?

20 great wines for as little money as possible

drink

Yering Station Frog Pinot Noir 2006
Yarra Valley
Australia

get it from...

£6.99

Majestic Wine Warehouse

Decent entry-level Pinot Noir has always been somewhat of an endangered species. After all, this is a demanding variety that demands you pour your heart, your soul, and, more than likely, your cash, into producing decent examples. It's heartbreaking stuff. Tom Carson knows a thing or two about producing decent Pinot Noir, and this example is right up to scratch. Sweet dark cherry, smoke, and spice fill the nose, while in your mouth Frog is soft, silky, and well structured – none of which is likely to break your heart.

Trentino-Alto Adige
Italy

Alois Lageder's brilliant entry-level Pinot Grigio pays homage to the local geology, once the site of an ancient underwater reef (hence the name: *Riff* is German for "reef"). Sourced from a blend of selected vineyards throughout Alto Adige, Trentino, and the Veneto, this wine represents seriously good value for money. Sporting a classic Grigio nose of honeysuckle, apple, river rock, and minerals, it's fresh, delicate, and squeaky clean. Lovely stuff.

get it from...

£8.99

Booths
WineTime
EWGA

Peter Lehmann Chenin Blanc 2007
Barossa Valley
Australia

PRODUCER OF THE YEAR

Team Peter Lehmann continues to deliver an astonishing range of wines across a full spread of price points. From the flagship Stonewell Shiraz (*see* page 124) all the way back to wines like this knockout summery white, rarely – if ever – do they disappoint. This is great Chenin: fresh, dry, and racy with plenty of citrus zip and zing. A closer look will unearth a nose of Granny Smith apples, lemon rind, and minerals, while in your mouth it's tight, dry, and crisp.

get it from...

£5.99

Booths
Budgens
Waitrose
Wine Cellar
Peter Lehmann Wines UK

get it from...

£7.99

Booths
Waitrose
James Nicholson Wine Merchant
Cambridge Wine Merchants
Vinites

Capçanes Mas Collet 2004
Montsant
Spain

There's a definite buzz about Montsant in southwest Catalonia. With prices in nearby Priorato reaching intergalactic levels, it's nice to know that, elsewhere, bargains aren't just a thing of the past. Garnacha, Tempranillo, Cariñena, and Cabernet Sauvignon – and much of it from old vines – provide a wine overflowing with cherry, blackberry, cedar, spice, and tobacco aromas, while in your mouth it's forward and generous, with a bright, mineral texture and a long, drying finish.

Banrock Station Shiraz / Mataro 2006
Riverina
Australia

For the past decade, Banrock Station has worked tirelessly to help restore wildlife habitats right around the planet. This straight-shooting, beautifully fruited blend of Shiraz and Mataro is a brilliant crowd pleaser, and guaranteed to keep your next crowd smiling. It's also worth remembering that part of the proceeds from the sale of every bottle will be donated to wetland conservation.

get it from...

£4.99

Sainsbury's
Tesco
Waitrose
Somerfield

get it from...

£5.49

Sainsbury's
Waitrose
Oddbins
Bacardi Brown-Forman

Martini Asti NV
Piedmont
Italy

Piedmont, in Italy's northwest corner, is home to some of the most breathtaking food-and-wine combinations on earth. Taken from selected growers throughout the Monferatto and Langhe hills, Moscato Bianco is the star of this show, so you can expect aromas of fresh grape juice, pear, and apple, while on your palate it's a little bit sweet, and ever-so-slightly fizzy. Unbeatable with a bowl of the freshest seasonal fruit you can find.

Let the Good Times Flow

*First appeared in *Waitrose Food Illustrated,* November 2006

Never take a bottle of wine you really want to drink to a party.

Don't get me wrong; not for a nanosecond am I suggesting you present your host, or guests, with ordinary wine – on the contrary. But, sadly, personal experience suggests that you arrive at a party, surrender your bottle in exchange for a luke-warm can of Carling, and that's probably the last you'll ever see of it. Heartbreaking stuff...

Party season is officially upon us, and whether it's a slap-up dinner with friends or the annual office blow-out, please, please, *please* spare a thought for that wine you're going to take – or simply, which wines you're going to serve over the coming festive period.

It shouldn't be difficult. And as a special note to the hosts: consider your event, consider your guests, consider the weather, and never, ever forget that you needn't spend a fortune in order to drink well.

Finally, be prepared. Have enough glassware, have enough ice, and most importantly, have enough wine! I very much doubt any leftovers will go to waste.

Bon Fiesta!

get it from...

£6.99

Sainsbury's
Waverley TBS
Hailsham Cellars
Stainton Wines
De Bortoli UK

De Bortoli Windy Peak
Pinot Noir 2006
Yarra Valley
Australia

Let's not muck around: the De Bortoli
stable of wines is vast – 25 different
brands (including casks) sourced from
a similar number of grape varieties and
regions. And, while much has changed
(and grown) since De Bortoli's
inception in 1928, this family-owned
operation has never forgotten that
great wine is made in the vineyard.
Whether you understand it or not,
partial hand-harvesting, some whole-
bunch fermentation, minimal filtration,
and lots of TLC are just some of the
many reasons why this bargain should
be on your next shopping list.

Errazuriz Estate Merlot 2005
Aconcagua
Chile

For all the mud that's been flicked at this variety and for every four-letter expletive that's been used against it, Merlot remains as popular as ever. And when it's this good, why shouldn't it be? From the moment you raise your glass, lush cassis and plum fruit uncontrollably flood your every sense. Characteristically, the palate is soft and forgiving with fresh acidity and fine-grained tannins. The perfect introduction to New World Merlot – and terrific value for money.

get it from...

£6.99

Sainsbury's
Tesco
Budgens
Oddbins
Thresher
Hatch Mansfield

Victoria Bitter NV
Abbotsford
Australia

As the hands-down most popular non-vintage Victorian sparkler among *The Juice* team, consistency seems the likely key to success here. How it tastes at the source should be exactly how it tastes on the other side of the world; I'm yet to be disappointed. Crown-sealed and deeply coloured, this offers a yeasty nose leading to a mouth-filling, yet bone-dry palate with balanced acidity, plenty of lively bubbles, and a great length of flavour. Also available in half-bottles.

get it from...

£25.92 (case of 24 x 37.5cl bottles)

Majestic Wine Warehouse

Cantine Leonardo da Vinci
Chianti 2005
Tuscany
Italy

get it from...

£6.49

Booths
Noel Young Wines
Roberson Wine Merchant
Villeneuve Wines
Liberty Wines

Co-ops once accounted for around 50 per cent of Italy's wine production, much of it sold off as blending material for some of the country's biggest brands. Many of the co-ops still remain, but much about their approach has changed. In the Tuscan village of Vinci, Cantine Leonardo da Vinci (named after the town's most famous resident) is one of Italy's more dynamic co-ops. Having concentrated efforts on the vineyards, the rewards have well and truly paid off here, with this lushly fruited and great-value red that is unmistakably Chianti.

Try new things. Some of the best value lies in lesser-known countries, varieties, and styles.

variety

St Hallett Poacher's Blend 2006
Barossa Valley
Australia

get it from...

£6.75

Bibendum Wine
The Fine Wine Company
Deakin Fine Wines

While English cricket-loving Matt Gant might have had little to smile about in recent times, away from the pitch there're plenty of reasons for him to be cheerful. Up until recently, Gant was the man charged with assembling this much-loved national treasure – where roughly two parts Semillon, one part Sauvignon Blanc, and a dash of Barossa Riesling blend to create a full-flavoured, long, citrus-tipped, dry white wine that's perfect for everyday drinking.

get it from...

£6.49

Sainsbury's
Tesco
Asda
Waitrose
Southcorp Wines

Lindemans Bin 50 Shiraz 2007
Multi-regional blend
Australia

I reckon I've been drinking this wine on and off for at least the last 13 years, and consistency is undoubtedly its key to success. It's not for keeping; in fact, the fresher the better in my opinion. Snap this wine up as soon as it hits the shelves and you'll be blown away by fresh, sweet, lifted raspberry and cherry fruit with plenty of bright pepper and spice.

Château Guiot Costières de Nîmes · Rosé 2006
Southern Rhône
France

"100 per cent Grenache with a few other bits and pieces thrown in," was the response I was offered from my good (but mathematically challenged) mate Dan when I asked what was in the gorgeous Guiot rosé. In fact, Grenache, Syrah, and Cinsault form this fuchsia-toned rosé from France's southern Rhône Valley. On the nose, there's plenty of redcurrant fruit together with bramble and spice, while the palate is rich, firm, and dry with focused acidity and a clean, dry finish. Heaven!

get it from...

£5.99

Majestic Wine Warehouse

Palacio de Bornos Verdejo 2006
Rueda
Spain

Not so many moons ago Verdejo was responsible for far more than its fair share of poorly made, highly oxidized wines. But much has changed, and this squeaky-clean example is representative of Rueda's new breed. Gooseberry, pear, and citrus-fruit aromas lead to a tight, crisp, lemony mouthful of wine. Super-clean, delicious, and insanely good value for money.

get it from...

£6.49

Waitrose
Mill Hill Wines
Vins de Bordeaux
C & D Wines

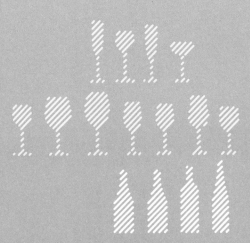

Guigal Côtes du Rhône Red 2004
Southern Rhône
France

get it from...

£7.99

Waitrose
Majestic Wine Warehouse
J E Fells & Sons

Lap swimming can be a mind-numbing pastime. I think about some random stuff as I trudge up and down my lane: for example, the average Olympic-sized swimming pool holds around 2.5 million litres of water, which translates into just over three million bottles of wine, which in turn works out to be the same amount of Côtes-du-Rhône rouge that Rhône superstar Guigal produces on average each year. Wow. The Guigals are fierce sticklers for detail, and it shows in this perennial medium-bodied, spicy southern Rhône fave.

get it from...

£5.49

Sainsbury's
J E Fells & Sons

Torres De Casta Rosado 2006
Catalonia
Spain

More than likely, you already know how good the wines of Torres are – particularly down the economy end of the ladder. From high in the hills of Penedès, this Catalonian powerhouse has carved a lively rosé with plenty of fresh berry fruit, vibrant acidity, and a finish that pulls up near enough to dry. Destined to become a summertime favourite – don't attempt to operate your barbeque without a bottle close by.

Nepenthe Sauvignon Blanc 2006
Adelaide Hills
Australia

The Adelaide Hills is home to some of Australia's most finely tuned cool-climate wines. And, with Sauvignon from this area firmly throwing down the challenge to the Kiwis, Nepenthe is one of the region's brightest stars. Expect a pale green, ultra-fresh wine loaded with gooseberry, elderflower, and blackcurrant alongside the kind of mouthwatering acidity that will guarantee you go back for more time and time again.

get it from...

£7.99

Sainsbury's
Enotria Winecellars

VILA VINITECA

Sweet Dreams
*First appeared in *Waitrose Food Illustrated,* February 2007*

Espai Sucre (Sugar Space) in Barcelona is one restaurant that takes its puddings very seriously indeed. And so it should – that's all they serve. The glucose deficient among you should be delighted to know that the jewel in Espai's crown is a five course degustation menu constructed entirely of sweet dishes – a specially crafted wine package to match is the icing on the cake. If like me you still dream about that scene in *Charlie and The Chocolate Factory* – the one where the golden ticket winners gorge themselves on trees made from spun sugar, animals from cake and water from chocolate – then Espai Sucre is about as close to food and wine Utopia as you and I are ever likely to get. But as mouth-watering (and calorific) as all that sounds, puddings pose a number of challenges for wine, and as a result great combinations are likely to require a bit more thought than normal. Often hurdles come in the form of extreme sweetness and tricky textures. My advice is to tackle sweet with sweet and try to match both the weight of your wine with the weight of your food as evenly as possible. Bearing these basic rules in mind, you shouldn't find yourself in too many sticky situations! Sorry…

Happy Drinking

get it from...

£7.99

Sainsbury's
Noel Young Wines
Wine by the Case
Cooden Cellars
Liberty Wines

Willunga 100 Grenache 2005
McLaren Vale
Australia

BARGAIN OF THE YEAR

This is a brilliant illustration of just how good Aussie wine at entry level can be – but sadly, all too often it's not. Here, Warren Randall's low-yielding, old-vine McLaren Vale Grenache coupled with Nick Haselgrove's experience at the helm has produced a wine which, right from the word go, has a nose full of old-vine fruit, offering true depth and spice, leading to a plush, inky palate loaded with sweet fruit and, above all else, value. Hands down Bargain of the Year!

Les Collines du Paradis
Minervois 2005
Languedoc
France

get it from...

£7.99

Tesco

Over the course of the past year, the sheer number of above-average wines hitting my desk from all corners of the Languedoc has been astounding. I welcome more with open arms! A chunky, rich blend of Syrah, Grenache, and Carignan – and drinking beautifully right now – this cracking wine is nothing short of a steal. A nose full of sweet plum, leather, and spice makes way for a dark, inky mouthful of fruit and some well-judged, chewy tannins.

Knowing what you like is a start, but knowing why you like it is what you should be aiming for.

know

Promessa Rosso Salento 2005
Puglia
Italy

Mark Shannon's Puglian estate, A Mano/Promessa has risen to become one of the true superstars of Italy's wine-producing south. A budget-conscious mix of Negroamaro and Primitivo – some of which is taken from old vines – this lushly fruited red is one of the wine world's last great bargains. Warm and layered spicy red fruit dominate the nose alongside aromas of bitter chocolate and amaro, while in your mouth it's forward and generous with vibrant acidity, chewy tannin, and great length of flavour. *Multo Buonissimo!*

get it from...

£5.75

Booths
Moriarty Vintners
Quaff Fine Wine Merchants
Bennetts Fine Wine Merchants
Liberty Wines

We have a global wine crisis on our hands. At the time of going to print, it's estimated that in Australia alone there's enough excess wine to pour around 7.5 billion glasses of the stuff. More worrying is that if the current backlog is not cleared, many producers will go to the wall and excess grapes could be processed into low-quality vinegar – or worse still, cheap fuel. So, the next time you have a reason to give, be it for love, money or just out of the goodness of your heart, spare a thought for the global wine industry and buy someone a bottle of wine.

20 great wines for giving – whatever the reason

give

Petaluma Croser Brut 2004
Adelaide Hills
Australia

get it from...

£14.95

Bibendum Wine
Wines of the World
Cellarworld

Brian Croser remains one of the most iconic and prolific figures within the international wine community. As founder of Petaluma, show judge, lecturer, businessman, visionary, strategist, and winemaker, he has provided knowledge and inspiration by the bucketload to many. With Croser's attention now fully focused on his Tapanappa venture, his final vintage at Petaluma was 2005. A blend of Champagne's major varieties, and made using the traditional method, the 2004 Croser is ripe and forward but still manages to juggle power with elegance effortlessly.

Anselmi I Capitelli
IGT Passito Bianco 2005
Veneto
Italy

Exhausted by regional red tape and
the complacency of many fellow
producers, the suave man of Soave,
Roberto Anselmi, decided to go it
alone in 2000 and re-label his wines
IGT Veneto rather than Soave DOC.
A modern sweet wine produced from
late-harvested Garganega grapes dried
on straw mats in a bid to concentrate
sugars, I Capitelli is insanely complex
and rich; even the nose explodes with
sweep ripe apricot, orange marmalade,
and spice.

get it from...

£27.00

Swig
Enotria Winecellars

Find a good wine shop.
It will cut out a lot
of the guesswork,
and (fingers crossed)
disappointment, too.

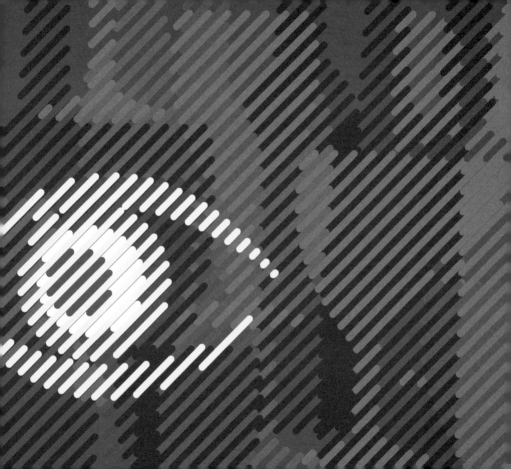

Ridge Geyserville Zinfandel 2004
California
USA

The legendary Paul Draper has been the man behind the controls at Ridge since 1969. The Geyserville vineyard produces a sleeping giant of a wine carved from 75 per cent old-vine Zin, 18 per cent Carignan, and 7 per cent Petit Syrah, and largely without intervention. And so what's it like? Hold on to your hats, these wines aren't for the faint of heart. Closer to black than purple in colour and densely concentrated, this is heavy artillery that should be kept in the cellar for the better part of the next decade.

get it from...

£25.00

Berry Brothers & Rudd
Philglas & Swiggot
Butlers Wine Cellar
HarperWells
Theatre of Wine
Fields, Morris & Verdin

Back to the Future

*First appeared in the *Herald Sun,* Melbourne / *Sunday Telegraph,* Sydney, February 2007

From skinny jeans to shell necklaces, this summer surf culture rolled back the years to circa 1981 and everything about Puberty Blues that used to make us laugh is now no longer a joke; even forking out for a pair of re-issue mid-thigh, pastel-toned board shorts – the very same ones I owned when I was nine – seemed like a good idea at the time. But, as common sense prevailed and the reality of just getting them on, let alone going for a swim, proved a bit much, one thing I was happy to have squeezed into this summer was plenty of R & R: that's Riesling and Rosé.

Sure, these two retro favourites might not be the coolest kids on the block, but they're certainly two of the most refreshing, food-friendly, and good-value drinks currently gracing the shelves of wine shops everywhere.

Beautiful bone-dry Aussie Riesling, with its mouthwatering acidity and insane flowery lime-juice purity: I've tried so many over the past few months that my teeth hurt! The BBQ got a proper seeing to also, and a summer's worth of ribs, wings, tentacles, and tails, together with plenty of sticky fingers, smoke, and fire meant that an icy bottle of good dry rosé was rarely out of reach.

get it from...

£11.50

Great Western Wine

Vincent Pinard Sancerre
"Cuvée Florès" 2005
Loire
France

As we continue to drown ourselves in a virtual ocean of New World Sauvignon Blanc, it would be very easy to forget that, not so long ago, it was the French who were having all the fun with this variety. Here's a perfect example of why. Lean, tight, and well-structured, the nose is all green apple, pear, and grassy smells, while in the mouth it's vibrant, zippy, and bone-dry. A textbook example from a great producer. Check it out.

Bay of Fires Arras 2000
Tasmania
Australia

Ed Carr, the don of Aussie fizz production, is back. As chief sparkling winemaker for Hardy, Carr is required to produce and oversee the production of numerous labels from Sir James right the way through to this year's *Juice* offering, Bay of Fires Arras. Carr and Co. are right on the money here, with a wine both superbly crafted and multi-layered. Citrus fruit, toast, and spice dominate the nose, while the palate is rich and intense, with plenty of small bubbles, cleansing acidity, and a clean, drying finish.

get it from...

£24.99

The Revelstoke Wine Company
Sheridan Coopers
Constellation

Ravenswood Belloni
Zinfandel 2000
California
USA

Since the mid-1970s, Ravenswood winemaker Joel Peterson – in his own unique style – has championed the cause for Zinfandel right around the planet. This red boasts a super colour, and the nose is perfumed, but still tightly bound up in pure, dark fruit, cedary oak, and exotic spice. On the palate, Belloni is mouth-filling, inky and rich, with a monster amount of clout which, bucking the general trend for Zin, will definitely benefit from a stint in a cool, dark spot for a couple of years.

Mitchelton Airstrip Marsanne / Roussanne / Viognier 2005
Goulburn
Australia

Marsanne, Rousanne, and Viognier: three varieties historically associated with France's Rhône Valley, but popping up with alarming frequency in other parts of the world, and in this case Australia. What you end up with is a full-bodied white whose aromatics range from white peach and apricot to orange rind, while in the mouth it's weighty, rich, and dry.

get it from...

£13.50

Bibendum
Wine by the Case

Katnook Founder's Block Cabernet Sauvignon 2004
Coonawarra
Australia

Punching well above its weight, Founder's Block displays the kind of spit and polish usually reserved for wines that go for far more money. Here Wayne Stehbens and Team Katnook deliver a serious mouthful of soft, sweet, blood-plum and cassis-like fruit, together with cleverly knit oak and soft and chewy Cabernet tannins. This wine is not only exceptional value for money, but a serious contender for "Bargain of the Year".

get it from...

£9.50

Bibendum Wine
Grapevine

Martín Códax Burgáns
Albariño 2005
Rías Baixas
Spain

Albariño (Alvariñho in Portugal and blending component for *vino verde*) is regarded by many as Spain's white grape *numero uno*. The cool, wet, and windy conditions of Galicia produce a wine with aromas of white peach and lime, while in your mouth Burgáns is soft, citrus-tipped, and pure. This is a brilliant introduction to Albariño, and yet another of Spain's growing white wine bargains.

get it from...

£8.99

Oddbins

Falesco Vitiano 2005
Umbria
Italy

By day, Ricardo Cotarella is one of Italy's superstar consultant winemakers. In what little spare time he has, Cotarella is the brains and muscle behind Falesco, his family estate in Umbria. Equal parts Cabernet, Sangiovese, and Merlot, Vitiano is a fruit-fresh everyday drinker. Production of this wine takes place in stainless-steel tanks followed by a short stint in oak. The result is a bright, medium-bodied red that well and truly over-delivers for the money.

get it from...

£6.80

New Generation Wines
Bristol Wine Company
Mill Hill Wines
Berkmann Wine Cellars

get it from...

£12.00

Swig
Enotria Winecellars

Planeta Cerasuolo di Vittoria 2006
Sicily
Italy

Few wineries south of Rome have managed to have the international impact of Planeta. Quite simply, they are the superstars of Italy's wine-producing south. Sourced from old-vine Nero d'Avola and Frappato, Cerasuolo is a deeply coloured yet super-fruity wine with masses of bright raspberry, blackberry, and spice. On the palate, prepare yourself for "lush" and "full", while bright acidity, cedary oak, and some fine, grippy tannin complete the picture.

get it from...

£13.50

The Secret Cellar
Fields, Morris & Verdin

Bonny Doon Syrah
"Le Pousseur" 2004
California
USA

It just wouldn't be right if we didn't include at least one wine from the "Temple of Doon". Le Pousseur is a user-friendly tongue-in-cheek screwcapped homage to the wines of France's Northern Rhône Valley. At the centre of this finely tuned wine lies a solid core of dark spicy plum, blackberry, and cedar, while in the mouth it's full, rich, and layered with sweet juicy fruit, dry grainy tannins, fresh acidity, and superb balance. Another class act from Randall Grahm.

Comtes Lafon Mâcon-Milly-Lamartine "Clos du Four" 2004
Burgundy
France

Burgundy is home to Dominique Lafon, possibly the most talented Chardonnay producer on Earth. Wines from his Meursault estate are some of the most sought-after in the world, but the good news for the rest of us is that he also makes a decent amount of affordable wine from the Mâcon which similarly bears his Midas touch. Expect restrained pear and citrus fruit alongside aromas of soft cashew and spice, while in your mouth it's minerally and restrained, with wicked length and great overall balance.

get it from...

£14.25

Fields, Morris & Verdin

Christmas Cheers
*First appeared in *Waitrose Food Illustrated*, December 2006

December 25 means a heavy day of over-indulgence. A day where slightly dotty family members will more than likely call you by the wrong name, a day when you're more than happy to be photographed in a fluorescent green tissue-paper crown, and a day when Dean Martin is king of the household CD player once more.

Don't get me wrong; I love Christmas. It's just the thought of all that eating and drinking that scares me to my very core. For hours after lunch we writhe around on the floor feeling uncomfortably full and wondering how on earth we've managed to put our bodies through it all again. I suspect this year will be no different. I'm already in training.

With so much happening on the table, Christmas lunch can be a tough assignment for wine. Take some time and consider what you're eating – structuring your menu properly is the key to keeping your guests feeling comfortable rather than stuffed.

Kick things off with a glass of bubbles to get tummies rumbling. Follow up with a well-chosen, user-friendly white and red for the main event, then finish the day off with a splash of something sweet and rich for the pudding.

Merry Christmas!

Antinori Guado Al Tasso Il Bruciato
Bolgheri 2003
Tuscany
Italy

Il Bruciato is a soft and early drinking Tuscan red from the coastal outpost of Italian powerhouse, Antinori. A tightly wound core of bitter cherry, plum, and leather sets the pace, while in your mouth soft, rich fruit is quickly followed by a wave of dry, grippy Cabernet tannins. Roping together Cabernet Sauvignon (60 per cent), Merlot (30 per cent), and Syrah (10 per cent), Il Bruciato is a stylish and affordable addition to the Antinori stable.

get it from...

£406 (12 bottle case price)

Fine & Rare Wines

get it from...

£13.99

Majestic Wine Warehouse
The Wine Society
Harrods
D Byrne & Co.
Maison Marques et Domaines

Casa Lapostolle Cuvée Alexandre Merlot 2005
Rapel
Chile

Casa Lapostolle knits Alexandra Marnier-Lapostolle's vision (and newly blinged-out winery) together with consultant oenologist Michel Rolland's know-how and some of the country's best parcels of Merlot. Hammered together in true Rolland style, CA Merlot is an essay in concentration and richness. Florescent purple in colour, this wine buzzes with sweet plum and milk chocolate, while a mouthful of dark, sweet, and inky fruit leads to a clean, dry finish. Such good value!

Terre del Poliziano Rosso di
Montepulciano 2005
Tuscany
Italy

get it from...

£8.99

Sainsbury's

Rosso di Montepulciano has long been
thought of as the poorer brother of
Vino Nobile di Montepulciano, but,
as is the case here, some Rosso's can
offer super value for money. A word
of warning – Vino Nobile and Rosso di
Monetpulciano are not to be confused
with Montepulicano d'Abruzzo which
is an altogether different grape variety
from an altogether different place.
Properly confused now? Good. From
a local version of Sangiovese,
Poliziano's Rosso sports a solid core
of pure, dark, cherryish fruit alongside
aromas of tobacco, earth, and spice.
In the mouth it's minerally and rich,
and rounded out by a wash of
trademark dry, grippy tannin. *Bellisimo!*

Baron Philippe de Rothschild
Escudo Rojo 2004
Maipo
Chile

Baron Philippe de Rothschild's
crowd-pleasing Chilean offering
continues to deliver smiles all round.
Escudo Rojo ("The Red Shield" –
which is what the Rothschild name
also means) is a medium-bodied
Cabernet-dominant blend from
Maipo, with plenty of stuffing and
nicely knit oak.

get it from...
£9.99

Costco
Selfridges & Co.
J E Fells & Sons

When buying wine in a shop or a restaurant, remember that the more specific you can be about what you do or don't want, the more likely you are to wind up with something you really like.

talk

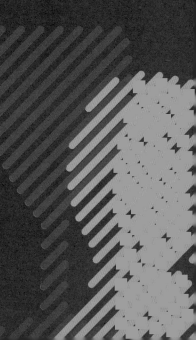

Kangarilla Road Shiraz 2004
McLaren Vale
Australia

get it from...

£9.99

Majestic Wine Warehouse

Almost like you might assemble a great big jigsaw puzzle, the fruit used in this wine is sourced from a combination of local vineyards ranging from cool to hot and high to low. Oak is a mixture of French and American, new and old. The results speak for themselves. There are aromas of sweet dark fruit, milk chocolate, and spice, while it's full and rich in the mouth, with terrific fruit intensity, vibrant acidity, and balanced drying tannins.

get it from...

£11.00

Berry Brothers & Rudd
Armit
Southcorp Wines

Penfolds Bin 138 Old Vine Barossa Valley Grenache / Shiraz / Mourvèdre 2004
Barossa Valley
Australia

It's generally considered that old vines, which become less productive with age, produce better-quality fruit. But one man's "old vines" are another man's "young vines", and this is where the problem starts. Fruit for this wine is sourced from vines ranging from 35 to 100 years in age. We're guessing more 35 than 100, but nevertheless, in 138 we find a concentrated wine with plenty of depth and purity that makes me think it might actually be more 100 than I imagined. A brilliant wine.

get it from...

£5.49

Nickolls & Perks
Halifax Wine Company
Andrew Chapman Fine Wines
Liberty Wines

Fairview Goats do Roam Red 2005
Paarl
South Africa

Having done much for the indigenous people of South Africa, Charles Back is one of the modern wine world's true heroes. Here, Back continues "tongue in cheek", paying homage to his beloved goats much to the irritation (you'd suspect) of producers in France's southern Rhône valley. This fruit-forward and brilliant everyday blend of Shiraz, Pinotage, and a little Cinsaut, Mourvèdre, Grenache, Merlot, Carignan, Gamay, and Cabernet (phew!) shouts bright raspberry, blood plum, pepper and spice, while in the mouth it's medium-bodied, soft, and dry.

Food, glorious food – and made even better by a well-chosen glass of wine. Like a romantic night in with the Mrs or Mr, food-and-wine matching shouldn't be an exercise saved only for special occasions, nor does it need to be expensive. Take some time and think about it: there's a match for just about everything. Have fun playing around with different combinations, but never let food-and-wine matching get in the way of simply enjoying something to eat and drink.

20 great wines that should be on your table

dine

Brown Brothers Liqueur Muscat NV
Rutherglen
Australia

My two best mates Tobie and Hayden got married earlier this year (not to one another, although it had been suggested...), and if ever there was a wine worthy of drinking with wedding cake, this is it. We're talking about a little slice of liquid history in a bottle here. Once a year, winemakers begin assembling the wine: some from the 40-year-old barrel, from the 30, the 20, and the 10-year-old, too. The results are spellbinding. Olive in colour, and with an amazing nose of dried citrus fruit, molasses, cinnamon, nutmeg, and clove, this wine is unctuous to taste, and rich with an insane length of flavour and heart-stopping depth and purity.

Ascheri Dolcetto d'Alba "Vigna Fontanelle" 2005
Piedmont
Italy

That breathtaking food and wine experiences are found on pretty much every corner in the town of Bra, is little surprise considering this is the spiritual home of the Slow Food movement. Dolcetto (little sweet one) sits third behind Nebbiolo and Barbera in Piedmont's red-grape hierarchy. Aromatically you get a pure core of cherry, raspberry, violet, and rose, while in the mouth it's lush and soft with dark mouth-filling fruit, dry chewy tannin, and good length. Risotto, with a couple of handfuls of the best wild mushrooms you can lay your hands on, will serve you perfectly.

get it from...

£8.49

Sainsbury's

Viña Santa Rita Reserva Sauvignon Blanc 2005
Casablanca Valley
Chile

If you've got more than just a few mouths to feed, then a whole fish – in this case steamed with capers, fennel, tomato, and olives – is a great option made better by well-priced, snappy dry whites such as this. Pale, almost water-like to look at, this is unmistakably Sauv Blanc. On the nose there's a stack of punchy gooseberry and blackcurrant fruit, while the palate is lean, tight, and racy with a mineral texture and razor-sharp acidity.

get it from...

£6.99

Majestic Wine Warehouse
D Byrne & Co.
Berkmann Wine Cellars

get it from...

£11.49

Peter Green
The Vineyard
Vinoteca Ltd
Alliance Wines

Domaine Albert Belle Crozes-Hermitage "Les Pierrelles" 2005
Northern Rhône
France

There's really only a few things more satisfying than a chargrilled, butterflied leg of lamb marinated in fennel and coriander seeds, garlic, lemon rind, and good oil. A perfect partner would be Albert Belle's excellent Les Pierrelles – a brilliant-value example of Syrah. This is finely tuned Crozes, where trademark raspberry, redcurrant, pepper, and spice lead the charge. In your mouth, Les Pierrelles is restrained, with a lovely mineral texture and a wash of supporting grippy tannin.

Kiwi Magic

*First appeared in the *Herald Sun*, Melbourne / *Sunday Telegraph*, Sydney, February 2007

Perched 70 metres (230 feet) above a narrow, rock-lined gorge, and with nothing more than a large rubber band separating you and mortality, I doubt there's a better time to ponder life's big questions than when they begin to count you down. Have I been a good person? *FIVE!* Am I happy with what I've achieved? *FOUR!* Have I lived life to the full? *THREE!* Did I treat everyone with respect? *TWO!* Am I wearing clean boxers? *GO!*

New Zealand Sauvignon Blanc is the liquid equivalent of bungee jumping. An adrenaline-fuelled assault on the senses which, in seconds, shocks, thrills, and yanks you back to reality, leaving you wondering what on earth just happened. Accounting for nearly 75 per cent of the country's total wine exports, you could also be forgiven for thinking it's all they make. You'd be wrong.

New Zealand – the cleanest, greenest country on earth – is also one of the wine world's most diverse. And, as Syrah and Merlot go from strength to strength up north, a fragile climate and poor soils provide an excellent starting point for Pinot Noir and a cast of whites in the south.

At the southern end of the North Island, Martinborough produces some of the best examples of Pinot Noir outside of Burgundy, while the South Island has made serious headway with aromatic whites. But most exciting in my opinion is Riesling. With one foot in the Old World and the other in the new, the racy Kiwi style straddles sweetness and acidity with precision and ease.

get it from...

£11.09

Croque-en-Bouche
Vinehaven
Berkmann Wine Cellars

René Muré Côte de Rouffach
Gewurztraminer 2005
Alsace
France

From the sun-soaked slopes of the Côte du Rouffach high up in the Vosges Mountains, this powerful and flamboyant Gewurz hits you with wave after wave of lychee, rosewater, musk, and ginger, while in the mouth, it's voluptuous, rich, full: effortlessly managing to be both big and beautiful all at once. A big salad of pork, prawn, and papaya from our legendary local Vietnamese, Song Que, remains our favourite Gewurz dish.

Champagne Larmandier-Bernier
Terre de Vertus Premier Cru NV
Champagne
France

The rise of independent Champagne growers like Larmandier-Bernier, Egly-Ouriet, and Jacques Selosse is a breath of fresh air for fizz-lovers everywhere. What sets these producers apart from the pack is a determination to capture a sense of place rather than to create the usual house-style. Carved from 50-year-old-plus, single-vineyard, Biodynamically grown Chardonnay vines, Terre de Vertus is a stunning wine with great poise, purity, and balance. Zero *dosage* only adds to the magic. A dozen of the freshest oysters you can find, served naturally, should do the trick.

Margan Family Botrytis Semillon 2007
Hunter Valley
Australia

The way to Mr. Skinner's heart was via one of the legendary Stephanie Alexander's famous lemon tarts complete with 13 eggs. Behind the winemaking controls of this estate, Andrew Margan produces some knock-out wines. This is a classic: concentrated aromas of botrytis and apricot lead to a sweet, rich, mouth-filling palate where bright acidity and a never-ending finish round out the equation. The perfect lemon tart wine.

get it from...

£10.99 (37.5cl)

Tanners Wine Merchants
Oxford Wine Company
Connolly's Wine Merchants
Charles Stevenson Wines
Siegel Wine Agencies

Livio Felluga Tocai Friulano 2005
Trentino-Alto Adige
Italy

get it from...

£16.95

Harvey Nichols
Nickolls & Perks
Halifax Wine Company
Liberty Wines

Great Japanese food requires wines with plenty of elegance and finesse, and the top right-hand corner of Italy is home to some of the most incredibly textural and fine white wines produced anywhere in the world. Produced from Tocai (not to be confused with Australian Tokay or Hungarian Tokáji) this wine from the Colli Orientali del Friuli DOC has a shy nose, with the slightest whiff of pear, lemon, sage, and minerals. On the palate, a steely mouthful builds into a long, acid-driven finish. Make sure you have a bottle with you during your next Sushi outing.

Marchesi de' Frescobaldi Chianti Rufina Riserva "Nipozzano" 2003
Tuscany
Italy

Census takers should hide their fava beans and hang on to their livers – this is great Chianti, although to be honest we think it's far better suited to Friday night pizza. Perched above Florence, Rufina is the smallest of the seven Chianti sub-zones, and offers a slightly leaner, tighter expression of Sangiovese than the more famous Chianti Classico. This version sports a solid core of pure, dark, cherryish fruit alongside aromas of fresh tobacco, earth, and spice. In the mouth, it's minerally, rich, and rounded-out by a wash of trademark dry Sangiovese tannin. I'm sure Hannibal Lector would approve.

get it from...

£12.49

Oddbins
Averys Wine Merchants
Hallgarten

get it from...

£26.95

Philglas & Swiggot
Valvona & Crolla
Moriarty Vintners
Andrew Chapman Fine Wines
Liberty Wines

Isole e Olena Vin Santo del Chianti Classico 1999
Tuscany
Italy

As one of my all-time favourite producers, what I really love about Isole e Olena is that while they stay true to the very traditional style of Sangiovese they deliver year in, year out, it's Paulo di Marchi's work with more international varieties such as Chardonnay, Syrah, and Cabernet Sauvignon that illustrate the true scale of his talents. *Vin santo* production is a proper labour of love. There are few great examples, but thankfully this wine sits on top of the pile. Watch it shine with bitter chocolate, dried fruit, or a slice or three of *Panforte*.

get it from...

£10.99

Sainsbury's
Tesco
Waitrose
Thresher
J E Fells & Sons

Warre's Otima 10-Year-Old Tawny Port
Douro
Portugal

Port is getting a long-overdue image makeover. Once the domain of crusty pin-striped men and their respective "boys clubs", port is thankfully reaching out to a younger, fresher audience. Otima 10-year-old is a recent addition to the Warre's camp. In the glass, the wine appears copper – almost rosé – in colour. The nose is a pretty mix of dried and candied fruit, sweet spice, nuts, and ground coffee. The palate is medium-bodied with a terrifically intense flavour, fresh acidity, and a long, clean finish that couldn't be a better partner to my mum's legendary chocolate slice if it tried.

Codorníu Reserva Raventós Cava Brut NV
Catalonia
Spain

There's something very liberating about fish and chips on the beach, toes in the sand, and wine in plastic cups. If you haven't done it in a while, rediscover it soon with a bottle of this excellent cava. For the better part of the last 500 years, Codorníu has been producing some stunning and brilliantly priced cavas. Following the same principals as those employed in the production of Champagne, this blend of Chardonnay, Xarel-lo, and Macabéo is loaded with ripe pear, green apple, honey, and brioche character, and is little short of a steal.

get it from...

£8.99

Majestic Wine Warehouse
Oddbins
Codorniu UK

Poggerino Chianti Classico 2004
Tuscany
Italy

get it from...

£11.95

Lea and Sandeman

If a two-inch-thick T-Bone, charred on the outside and rare in the middle, sounds like your cup of tea, then make the pilgrimage to Panzano in Chianti and have the great Dario Ceccini cook it for you at his low-key local trattoria. A bottle of Poggerino is essential company. Piero and Benedetta Lanza own and run this small Radda-based estate, and are part of the new guard of Tuscan winemaking turning out modern, richly fruited wines without sacrificing varietal or regional integrity. This is stylish and unmistakable Sangiovese (with a small percentage of Merlot), sporting a nose full of morello cherrry, leather, and tobacco. Taste-wise, it's plush, mineral-textured, and framed by trademark fine, chalky tannins and a clean, dry finish.

DEGUSTACIÓ
VINS · LICORS
EMBUTITS IBÈRICS
FORMATGES

Lustau East India Solera NV
Jerez
Spain

Many moons ago, and in a time long before refrigerated shipping, barrels of sherry bound for the Indies were lashed to ships (partly as ballast, but more likely for easy access), exposed to the full fury of Mother Nature. It was discovered that the intense heat encountered during these journeys often resulted in the positive development of the wines – hence the now very deliberate production of Lustau East India sherry. Think aromas of toffee, molasses, Middle Eastern spices, nuts, and dried fruits, and you begin to get the picture. Make sure it's on your table this Christmas Day.

Heyl zu Herrnsheim Baron Heyl Riesling Spätlese 2004
Rheinhessen
Germany

get it from...

£12.45

Armit

With holdings spread across the *Roter Hang*'s ("Red Slope") most famed vineyards, together with increasing employment of ecologically sound and sustainable practices, the Heyl zu Herrnsheim estate is internationally regarded as one of Germany's finest exponents of Riesling. Tightly sprung with amazing depth and purity, the palate shows incredible intensity, power, and youth along with a stunning balance between sweetness and acidity. This year's Friday night favourite has been homemade Thai fishcakes with lemon and sea salt – great Riesling food!

It's a Knockout
*First appeared in *Waitrose Food Illustrated*, April 2007

When Muhammad Ali stepped into the ring to face George Foreman in 1974's historic "Rumble in the Jungle", he squared up every inch the underdog. Despite the fact the two fighters were virtually the same weight, Foreman had size on his side, not to mention sheer "punch your lights out" power. Ali, on the other hand, had technical skill, speed, elegance, and individuality. Foreman was the 8-to-1 favourite when the bell rang for the first time. The rest, as they say, is history.

We live in an age where a lot of wine is made by numbers, where individuality is either thin on the ground or frowned upon and – worst of all – where a mouthful of sheer "punch your lights out power" is often seen as a good thing.

A friend who runs a wholesale wine business in London recently commented that "the emphasis should be on the quality of a wine rather than fleshing out a marketing budget". Hear! Hear! But surely that's just par for the course? You'd be surprised; I taste way more bland and ordinary wine than you'd ever care to know about.

The good news though is that, even in the most crowded of tasting line-ups, individuality, elegance, and, above all else, quality, stand out like an Ali right hook.

Enate Rosado Cabernet Sauvignon 2006
Somontano
Spain

Halfway between Barcelona and Pamplona lies the modern and extremely angular headquarters of Enate. From its stables comes a rosé to think about. I mean, this is the kind of rosé – produced entirely from Cabernet Sauvignon for its depth and structure – that I could happily sit with rather than guzzle. Redcurrant, wild berry, and rosehip notes on the nose are followed by a palate that is rich, mineral-textured, fine, chewy, and dry. A pile of chargrilled sourdough, Jamon Iberico, and good oil, is just about all you'll need for a great Saturday lunch. I say just about because you'll need a bottle of this also...

get it from...

£8.99

Averys Wine Merchants
Hallgarten

Chryseia 2004
Douro
Portugal

Slap bang in the midst of a major table-wine revolution, Portugal is producing some stunning wines – but not for the faint of heart! A full-blown blend of Touriga Franca, Touriga Nacional, and Tinta Cão, Chryseia is about as close as I've come to finding the vinous equivalent of Metallica. Jet black, and from the moment you stick your nose in the glass, full on and unrelenting. I love it! Everybody has their own idea of the perfect burger – mine is an "Aussie" – complete with egg, bacon, beetroot, and the works. Perfect alongside one of Portugal's new wave reds.

get it from...

£29.99

Tanners Wine Merchants
Harrods
Wimbledon Wine Cellars
J E Fells & Sons

Yering Station ED
Pinot Noir Rosé 2006
Yarra Valley
Australia

Much as we love residual sugar in
our German Riesling, ED (Extra Dry)
is how we prefer our rosé thank you
very much. Here, Tom Carson and his
team have cut out a wine that is near
enough to salmon in colour, while
a big sniff will reveal a pared-back
nose of wild strawberry, redcurrant,
and herbs. On the palate, ED Pinot
Rosé manages to be delicate, pretty,
and light before clamping on the
brakes with a lick of tannin and
lively acidity. We couldn't get enough
of this wine with pan roasted salmon,
spring greens, and a big dollop of
crème fraîche.

get it from...

£11.50

Enotria Winecelllars
Australianwinesonline.com

Visit a vineyard. That doesn't mean you have to go on a "wine holiday", but there's something pretty special about drinking wine with the person who made it in the place where it was made.

travel

Evans & Tate X&Y
Chardonnay 2006
Margaret River
Australia

get it from...

£8.99

HwCg

Chardonnay – such as this excellent
X&Y – and roast chicken is one of
those matches made in heaven – they
were just meant to go. At street level,
good-value Chardonnay is thin on the
ground. Don't believe me? Wander into
pretty much any supermarket and
prepare yourself for row after row of
soulless, formulaic, sweet, oak-ridden
muck – no wonder most of us turn up
our noses at even the slightest
mention of it. Chardonnay deserves
better. Here you get restrained citrus
fruit on the nose coupled with the
faintest whiff of wood, while in your
mouth it's elegant and fine. This is a
giant step in the right direction.

get it from...

£5.95

O W Loeb & Co.
WoodWinters Wines & Whiskies

Innocent Bystander Pink Moscato 2007
Yarra Valley
Australia

Phil Sexton is forever innovating. His Innocent Bystander range has produced a string of great releases since its launch some years back. Perhaps the most exciting, though, is this Moscato, complete with crown seal. Pale-pink in colour it has a fresh and pretty nose of grape juice, pear, and spice – and much less manufactured than some of its Northern hemisphere cousins. The palate is fresh and delicate, with gentle fizz, grapey sweetness, bright acidity, and a lick of tannin to clean it all up. Serve this at the end of your next dinner party with the best strawberry and lemon Gelati you can lay your hands on.

Every now and again it's okay, even healthy, to blow a bit more than usual on something really special. Remember that, with wine, you generally get what you pay for and, in the case of the following wines, super attention to detail, tiny productions, and well-earned reputations count for everything. Throughout the coming pages, you'll find 20 "try before you die" kind of wines – although let's hope that's not for some time. Keeping in mind that you may have to look a bit harder than normal to find a few of the wines in this chapter, I hope you fall in love with them once you do.

20 great wines worth blowing the rent on

splurge

Peter Lehmann Stonewell
Shiraz 2001
Barossa Valley
Australia

PRODUCER OF THE YEAR

Taken from premium old-vine low-yielding vineyards throughout the Barossa, Stonewell 2001 bares all the hallmarks of a long, dry growing season – and is one of the best Stonewells I've tasted to date. Having done a near about-face on the oak front, as well as toning down the overall intensity of fruit, what this wine sacrifices in power, it gains in finesse. Although still incredibly concentrated, it has terrific purity of fruit and perfectly integrated cedary oak. Definite special-occasion stuff.

get it from...

£32.99

Waitrose
Oddbins
Noel Young Wines
Sunday Times Wine Club
Peter Lehmann Wines UK

F. E. Trimbach Riesling
Clos Ste Hune 2001
Alsace
France

get it from...

£75.00

The Wine Society
Harrods
Selfridges
Fortnum & Mason
Paragon

Open the dictionary and take a peek under the word "Riesling". What does it say? "Trimbach". No, that's not true, although Trimbach is one of the finest exponents of this grape variety anywhere, and this, its single-vineyard flagship, is a knockout. Clos Ste Hune is a walled *monopole* (a solely owned vineyard). The wall is significant because it protected the vines within from that pesky vine louse, phylloxera. With production rarely exceeding more than 600 cases, this is pure, dry, mineral-edged Riesling that has incredible depth and purity.

The Pinotphile

*First appeared in the *Herald Sun,* Melbourne / *Sunday Telegraph,* Sydney, March 2007

"You're deranged, Skinner."

It's fair to say that my mate Mike was clearly distressed by what he'd just heard.

"You're telling me you flew 20,000km (12,427 miles) to New Zealand to be with 500 fellow wine geeks for a four-day conference on a single grape variety? That's not normal behaviour. I don't get it."

At this point you should know that Mike is a football-loving, lager-swilling Londoner. A lovely guy. But to be honest, I never expected him to get it.

That single grape variety was Pinot Noir – a grape variety with the capacity to make us do strange and irrational things. In the film *Sideways*, character Miles sums up Pinot Noir beautifully: "It's a hard grape to grow. It's thin-skinned, temperamental, ripens early. It's not a survivor like Cabernet, which can just grow anywhere and thrive even when it's neglected. No, Pinot needs constant care and attention.

"And, in fact, it can only grow in these really specific, little tucked-away corners of the world. And only the most patient and nurturing of growers can do it. Only somebody who really takes the time to understand Pinot's potential can then coax it into its fullest expression."

It just so happens that Australia is one of those really specific, little tucked-away corners of the world. Some great Pinot Noirs come from the Mornington Peninsula, Yarra Valley, Macedon, and Tasmania. And remembering that we're not talking about a variety that's cheap to produce, expect to pay a bit more than normal.

get it from...

£40.95

Brokenwood Graveyard
Vineyard Shiraz 2004
Hunter Valley
Australia

Brokenwood began life in 1970 as a weekend refuge for wine-loving solicitors James Halliday, Tony Albert, and John Beeston. With the inclusion of the company flagship wine "Graveyard Shiraz" in *Langton's Classification of Australian Wines*, Brokenwood has today grown to become one of Australia's most iconic brands. This single-vineyard Shiraz ticks all the right boxes: great colour, a nose of blackcurrant, plum, cedar, pepper, and spice and a voluptuous, sweet, and long mouthful of fruit.

Bell Hill Pinot Noir 2005
Canterbury
New Zealand

get it from...

£34.95

Lay & Wheeler

Further strengthening New Zealand's reputation as the measuring stick for New World Pinot Noir, Bell Hill was established by Marcel Giesen and Sherwyn Veldhuizen in 1997 with the aim of creating wines that captured the full expression of their vineyards, rather than ones which emulated those from another part of the world. To date, a variety of clones and rootstocks planted at high density across a mix of sites have produced some of the most exciting examples of Pinot Noir to emerge from this side of the equator in recent memory. Pinot Noir lovers – if it means walking over hot coals in order to get your hands on these incredible wines – do it.

NB. The bottle image is of the equally good 2004 vintage.

Californian wine merchant Kermit Lynch brought Domaine Tempier to the attention of the modern world in his classic book *Adventures on the Wine Route*. Located on the south coast of France halfway between Marseille and Toulon, Tempier produces five terroir-driven *cuvées* of old-vine Mourvèdre, one white wine, and perhaps the world's greatest rosé. Produced from a mix of Mourvèdre, Grenache, and Cinsault, and with only a tiny amount of time in contact with the skins, the result is a clean, fruit-fresh, dry, and grippy rosé that you definitely need to try.

get it from...

£160.00 (*en primeur*)

Fine & Rare Wines
WinePro
Bordeaux Index

Château Léoville-Las-Cases 2000
Bordeaux
France

Dynasty after dynasty, generation after generation, the story of Léoville-Las-Cases – perhaps *the* most famous of Bordeaux's "super seconds" – is like an entire season of *Days of our Lives* (both Léoville-Barton and Léoville-Poyferré were born out of the Las-Cases division). With Cabernet Sauvignon the soul and backbone of the Left Bank, expect wave after wave of pure blackcurrant fruit and tight-knit, cedary oak. Merlot, Cabernet Franc, and Petit Verdot round out the equation.

Kistler Dutton Ranch
Chardonnay 2002
California
USA

Californian Chardonnay doesn't come much better than Kistler – and that's almost selling these wines short. In fact, Kistler's range of single-vineyard Chardonnays is world-class, effortlessly knitting New World richness with Old World structure and charm. On the nose you get all kinds of amazing aromas such as crème brûlée, cashew, grapefruit, nectarine, and pork crackling, while in your mouth it's rich and intense, with minerally texture and a jaw-dropping length of flavour. With its tiny production, a needle in the haystack search will almost certainly be required, but for the lucky few who manage to get their hands on a bottle, you won't be disappointed.

Vasse Felix Heytesbury Red 2002
Margaret River
Australia

Bizarrely, Vasse was a Frenchman who drowned exploring the Western Australian coastline, while *felix* is the Latin word for luck!? Not in my book. Anyhow, drawing fruit from Margaret River and Mount Barker, Heytesbury is a full-throttle Cabernet-Sauvignon-based wine incorporating small amounts of Shiraz, Malbec, and Merlot into the mix. Super colour leads to a nose flooded with lifted blackcurrant, ripe, juicy plums, dark chocolate, and sweet, cedary oak. In your mouth Heytesbury is full, inky, and perfectly formed.

get it from...

£30.09

Selfridges
Wimbledon Wine Cellar
Australian Wines Online
Berkmann Wine Cellars
Negociants

Kracher "Nouvelle Vague"
Grande Cuvee
Trockenbeerenauslese No. 7 2002
Burgenland
Austria

Alois Kracher is one of the greatest
sweet-wine producers in the world.
Situated on the botrytis-friendly
banks of Lake Neusiedl on the Austro-
Hungarian boarder Kracher creates
a handful of traditional, and not so
traditional (Nouvelle Vague) sweet
wines. From the not-so-traditional
camp, this wine is full and rich with
concentrated apricot, orange rind,
quince, and honey on the nose.
The palate is sweet and tropical,
but knockout acidity adds balance
to an otherwise super-charged
mouthful of wine.

get it from...

£27.99

Fortnum & Mason
Harvey Nichols
Wimbledon Wine Cellar
Philglas & Swiggott
Noel Young

Domaine Auguste Clape
Cornas 2004
Northern Rhône
France

get it from...

£33.00

Yapp Brothers

There are some wines you really look forward to tasting and then, on an altogether different level, there are those that almost make you sick with anticipation: proper butterflies-in-the-stomach, first-date nerves. For me, Clape Cornas is one of these wines. Rarity aside, this is one of the finest expressions of Syrah produced anywhere in the world. Pure, dark, and tightly wound Syrah with leather, earth, firm tannin, vibrant acidity, and a very strong will to live! Stash a few bottles in the cellar and forget about them for the better part of a decade.

get it from...

£323.00 *(en primeur)*

Corney & Barrow

Domaine de la Romanée-Conti La Tâche Grand Cru 2005
Burgundy
France

You might appreciate the difficulty of summarizing an estate such as DRC in fewer than 80 words. In short, this domaine is the benchmark upon which all other estates in Burgundy (and beyond) are measured. It's the most famous, and probably the greatest, estate in Burgundy today. This is Pinot Noir's Holy Grail within its Holy Grail. La Tâche, a *monopole* vineyard, produces wines which at best are multi-layered, insanely pure, slightly animal, incredibly textural, seductive, slinky, fine and, most of all, magic.

Château Coutet Premier Cru 2001
Bordeaux
France

Barsac-based Coutet has always been killer value for money. A racy mix of Sémillon and Sauvignon Blanc, this wine often comes across a bit lighter and fresher than many examples from neighbouring Sauternes, while still remaining pure and well-balanced. Citrus fruit, marmalade, quince, and spice hum away on the nose, while in your mouth you get amazing concentration of flavour that's lifted beautifully by fresh and vibrant acidity. Check it out.

get it from...

£29.00 (37.5 cl; *en primeur*)

Fine & Rare Wines
Bibendum Wine

Gaja Barbaresco 2003
Piedmont
Italy

There is no other way to put it: this is *the* vinous equivalent of the Bugatti Veyron 16.4. It's a powerful, slick, and hand-crafted wine by one of the wine world's true stars, Angelo Gaja. The Gaja estate in Barbaresco produces wines of great depth and substance, but never at the expense of regional character. The star of the show is a powerful and multi-dimensional expression of Nebbiolo that can swallow up vast amounts of new oak while still managing to retain elegance and charm by the bagful.

get it from...

£720.00 (12-bottle case price)

Armit

get it from...

£29.99

Waitrose
Harrods
Harvey Nichols
Hailsham Cellars
Louis Latour

Craggy Range Le Sol Syrah 2004
Hawke's Bay
New Zealand

You'd expect that at least some of Hawke's Bay's Cabernet and Merlot will make excellent barbecue fuel this summer, given the recent flurry of well-deserved praise for the area's efforts with Syrah. At Craggy Range, Steve Smith, MW, and team produce a muscular, meaty style of Syrah with huge presence and personality. Deep purple, the nose overflows with sweet dark plums, violets, ground coffee, roasted meat, and sweet spice, while in the mouth, it's full and firm, with cedary oak and some chewy tannin to finish.

get it from...

£26.40

Tanners Wine Merchants

Burgundy
France

This is Chablis of monumental proportions. It's all here – the river rock, the mineral, the lemon and green apple, the honey and hay. This is what I long for every time I pull the cork on a bottle of Chablis, but don't always get. Vincent Dauvissat, together with sparring partner François Raveneau, has been referred to as one of the "twin gods" of Chablis, their influence spawning a new generation of quality-conscious producers in the district.

Formula for Fun

*First appeared in the *Herald Sun,* Melbourne / *Sunday Telegraph*, Sydney, March 2007

I have this recurring dream where I'm driving in a grand prix. I think it's Monaco (of course it is) and I've just hit the lead. Alonso, Montoya, Fisichella…even fellow countryman Mark Webber are little more than dots in my rear-view mirror. But then, with just seconds to go as I'm hammering toward the chequered flag, I run out of petrol. With a bit of help pushing, I finish dead last.

Start your engines people: it's race day! And at approximately 4.10pm this afternoon, with a new Australian F1 champion crowned, roughly 9 litres (2.3 gallons) of Mumm Champagne will be sprayed onto the thirsty pit crews below. It's a tradition that dates back to the 1960s, when, as a sign of his appreciation, Dan Gurney (having just won Le Mans and not speaking much French) did the next best thing and proceeded to empty his winning bottle of Moët onto his crew. Excluding Islamic Bahrain, and barring tragedy, it's a tradition that's sticks to this day.

And so, with bubbles the theme, it's worth bearing in mind that the quality of Australian sparkling wine has never been better. Victoria's Yarra Valley has long been a favourite of sparkling wine producers, while across Bass Strait, Tasmania is now recognized as the premium source of top-drawer, sparkling fruit.

Vega-Sicilia Único 1991
Ribera del Duero
Spain

Tempranillo, Cabernet Sauvignon, Merlot, and Malbec join forces to form not just one of Spain's, but one of the world's truly great wines. Founded in 1864, Vega-Sicilia's top *cuvée,* Único, is aged in a variety of oaks (old, new, big, and small) for a whopping 10 years on average. And, while dense, dark fruit, leather, and sweet spice dominate the nose, oak plays less of a role in the final product than you might imagine – testament to the skill of this amazing estate.

get it from...

£146.00

Harrods
The Secret Cellar
WoodWinters Wines & Whiskies
Fields, Morris & Verdin

get it from...

£88.00

The Vineyard Cellars

In 1968, the late Al Brounstein purchased an 80-acre plot of land on Diamond Mountain, Calistoga, Napa Valley, with the sole intention of planting vines. Today, with just Cabernet Sauvignon in the ground, Diamond Creek produces four brilliant and distinctly different wines from four very different terroirs. Of these, the 8-acre dry-farmed Volcanic Hill vineyard produces some of the most powerful and long-lived, deeply concentrated wines with blackberry, cassis, and mineral aromas. In the mouth, it's inky and full, with bright acidity, cedary oak, and dry, chewy tannins.

Domaine Ramonet Chassagne-Montrachet Premier Cru Morgeot 2005
Burgundy
France

The rugby-loving Noel Ramonet handcrafts some of the most amazing examples of Chardonnay produced anywhere. From the minuscule one-acre Morgeot vineyard, this is iron-fist/silk-glove Chardonnay that blazes with grapefruit-citric intensity, pork rind, gun-smoke, mineral, cashew, and spice from the moment it hits your lips. An explosive citrus-driven mouthful of wine continues to reverberate long after you've swallowed it – indication of just how good this producer is.

get it from...

£300.00 (12-bottle case price; *en primeur*)

Berry Brothers & Rudd
O W Loeb & Co.
Direct Wines

Agricola Punica Barrua 2004
Sardinia
Italy

WINE OF THE YEAR

The rise of southern Italy has been well-documented over the past couple of years, but perhaps the most exciting chapter in the story so far has been the arrival of Barrua: the first superwine from "The New South". Punica is a joint venture between Tuscan superstars Tenuta San Guido, Sardinian powerhouse Cantina Sociale di Santadi, oenologist Sebastiano Rosa, consultant oenologist Giacomo Tachis, and Antonello Pilloni. Made from old-vine Carignan, and Merlot to fill in the blanks, Barrua is immediate. Masses of dark, sun-drenched fruit and spice flood your nose, while a mouthful reveals a lush, inky wave of ripe, dark fruit, spicy new oak, and a wash of dry, grippy tannins.

get it from...

£30.00

Swig
Enotria Winecellars

Torbreck Cuvée Juveniles 2006
Barossa Valley
Australia

A household name among Aussie wine lovers, Torbreck has set the pace for seriously concentrated old-vine wines from the Barossa. Made from massively concentrated fruit that comes off vines ranging from 40 to 150 years old, Juveniles was first made exclusively for Tim Johnston's legendary Parisian wine bar, "Juveniles". An unwooded blend of Grenache, Shiraz, and Mourvèdre (here called Mataro), this wine has heaps of bright raspberry and cherry fruit and is designed to drink young, but will hold on for a few years yet should you have the self-discipline to wait.

get it from...

£15.99

Fortnum & Mason
The Wine Library
Longford Wines
The Manor Cellars
Bordeaux Wine Investments
HBJ

Do a wine course – it's a small investment considering how much you're likely to spend on wine over the course of your drinking life.

Got a few bottles hidden under the bed, next to the boiler, on top of the fridge or in the boot of your car? Shame on you! Wine is a living, breathing thing, and while not all wine gets better with age, many transform into amazing old creatures, given time and, most importantly, the right conditions. You don't have to spend a fortune on wines to stick away, nor do you need a cellar. Find somewhere cool, dark, and away from vibration – the cupboard under the kitchen sink isn't going to cut it here. And if you struggle in the self-discipline department, a padlock might come in handy too …

20 great wines worth sticking away

stash

get it from...

£7.99

Averys Wine Merchants
Armit
Hailsham Cellars
Matthew Clark
Southcorp Wines

Wynns Coonawarra Estate Riesling 2004
Coonawarra
Australia

Hands down, one of the best-value examples of Riesling in Australia – and the latest offering from Coonawarra is par for the course. These wines continue to stuff a huge amount of content into their skeletal Coonawarra framework. Wynns is packed with pure lemon-lime citrus fruit, spice, and biscuit notes on the nose, while on the palate, the wine is rich and limey with nicely bound acidity and a bone-dry finish. And while it's drinking beautifully now, hide a couple of bottles with the aim of finding them in a decade or so.

Leeuwin Art Series Margaret River
Chardonnay 2004
Margaret River
Australia

We'd prefer not to weigh into whether
this may or may not be Australia's
greatest Chardonnay, but rather point
out that this wine sports a serious
reputation for longevity. Alongside
superb structure, Leeuwin is clean,
pure, and precise. Slick citrus and
stone fruit and restrained nutty oak
dominate much of what you smell,
while the palate unwinds with
minerally precision and disappears
off into the sunset with an amazing
length of flavour.

get it from...

£40.00

Harvey Nichols
Luvians Bottleshop
Philglas & Swiggot
Wimbledon Wine Cellar
Domaine Direct

Craiglee Shiraz 2004
Sunbury
Australia

get it from...

£20.00

D Byrne & Co.
Raffles Fine Wines

As one of my all-time-favourite Aussie wines, Craiglee Shiraz bucks the trend for super-charged, oak-driven beasts, and leans heavily on elegance and finesse – the keys to this wine's incredible ability to age. Lovingly assembled by the humble and talented Pat Carmody, dark-plum and sour-cherry fruit backed by trademark pepper and spice continue to define a wine that consistently reflects both the year in which it was grown and variety from which it was made. Do yourself a favour and hop on the mailing list.

Seghesio Family Vineyards
Sonoma Zinfandel 2005
California
USA

The Seghesio story begins in Piedmont, Italy, with Eduardo Seghesio heading for the USA in search of a better life. Drawn to northern Sonoma County, Seghesio set about constructing his own winery, and in 1902, Seghesio Vineyards – mainly planted with a mix of Italian varietals – was born. With the younger generation of the family now at the helm, Zinfandel, Cabernet Sauvignon, and Chardonnay have been much of the focus. Sourced from largely old-vine material, this is deeply concentrated wine, with layer-upon-layer of fruit and oak.

get it from...

£15.95

Booths
Harrods
Noel Young Wines
Virgin Wines
Liberty Wines

get it from...

£7.49

Sainsbury's
Somerfield
Thresher
Constellation

Leasingham Clare Valley Magnus Riesling 2005
Clare Valley
Australia

Riesling has an uncanny ability to age. Fresh citrus character that's so obvious in young examples, such as this Magnus, makes way for honeyed – almost keroseine-like – wines of huge depth. The team at Leasingham has long been turning out some of the Clare Valley's most consistently brilliant and affordable wines. This really is textbook stuff. The nose is explosive and bright, with lime juice, mandarin, fresh-cut flowers, and spice, while inside your mouth this wine just unleashes citrus fruit so pure, so long, and so well-balanced, it'll make your want to cry – literally. Have the tissues on standby.

get it from...

£30.00

Armit
Noel Young Wines
Southcorp Wines

Wynns Coonawarra Estate
Michael Shiraz 2004
Coonawarra
Australia

For many large-scale commercial operations, quantity usually comes at a price; not here. From ridiculously good (and cheap) Riesling (*see* page 156) to this flagship Shiraz, winemaker Sue Hodder is nothing short of a magician. Concentrated, inky, and dense, the nose is loaded with aromas of dark plum, pepper, and spice. The palate is weighty and full on, with loads of fruit and brilliant structure. Best of all, the oak has been dealt out sparingly. This is a monster that you could happily put in the cellar and forget about for the next 20 years or so.

Domaine de la Vougeraie
"Terres de Famille"
Bourgogne Rouge 2004
Burgundy
France

get it from...

£14.25

Fields, Morris & Verdin

Pascal Marchand's entry-level Pinot
Noir is a crystal-clear illustration of the
Vougeraie house style. And, as great
as these wines are, rarely (if ever) do
they long for fruit and oak. Not every
Pinotphile's cup of tea, but far from a
bad thing, particularly in the case of
entry-level Pinot. Deep, cherry-red to
look at, this wine has a nose that is all
wound up with underlying cherry,
violet, and spice aromas.On the
palate you'll find that it's silky, fine,
and balanced by some nice dry,
grippy tannin.

Domaine Billaud-Simon
Chablis 2005
Burgundy
France

Where many examples of Chardonnay
come apart at the seams after only a
few years in bottle, great Chablis more
often goes the other way. Ancient
Kimmeridgian soils, a super-cool
climate, and the stunning vintage that
was 2005 have produced some
amazingly pure and fine expressions
of Chablis. Made from 100 per cent
Chardonnay and with zero oak
influence, Billaud-Simon Chablis 2005
is an essay in balance and freshness
from one of the region's finest
producers. Here you'll find a nose full
of honeysuckle, pear, river rock, and
cashew, while the palate is tightly
wound and delicate, with soft stone
fruit and a mineral texture. Superb.

get it from...

£10.00

The Wine Society
Montrachet Fine Wines
The Ledbury Wine Cellar

J.TORRES Petit
1.751 – 1.814

All that Glitters

*First appeared in *Herald Sun,* Melbourne / *Daily Telegraph*, Sydney, April 2007

Oliver Stone's *Wall Street* was the epitome of 80s excess – a movie that documented the good, the bad, but mainly the ugly aspects of an era many of us would rather forget. Just in case you'd forgotten, this was a period when we wore shoulder pads, danced like robots, worshipped Madonna, and drank so much Chardonnay that 20 years on we can barely bring ourselves to even say the word. For those still keeping their distance – relax – it's alright to drink Chardonnay again.

In an effort to woo a new audience, and reassure an old one, Chardonnay – like Madonna – has been made over. Gone is the heavy-handed use of oak, the super-sized tropical fruit, and the "everything but the kitchen sink" approach to winemaking. The new face of Aussie Chardonnay is leaner and more focussed than ever before, and as a result these are wines far better balanced, better suited to food, and more adequately equipped to go the distance in the cellar. Best of all, these are wines that, in most cases, you'd happily drink more than just a glass of.

get it from...

£150.00

Berry Brothers & Rudd
Selfridges & Co.
Harvey Nichols
Harrods
House of Fraser
Maison Marques et Domaines

Champagne Louis Roederer
Cristal 2000
Champagne
France

Founded in 1776, the Champagne house of Louis Roederer has an uncompromising approach to quality and style – producing wines that age incredibly well. Cristal was created specifically for Czar Alexander II, who requested his Champagne be bottled in clear crystal bottles; and only Pinot Noir and Chardonnay from the 10 most celebrated Roederer *crus* are used in the production of this wine. Expect Champagne with all the complexity and finesse of great white Burgundy, and with the hip-hop fraternity having moved onto Dom Pérignon and Krug Rosé, maybe that means there'll be more to go around? I doubt it…

Penfolds Yattarna Chardonnay 2004
Multiregional blend
Australia

Yattarna is the result of Penfolds' very deliberate quest to produce a white wine rivalling the quality and prestige of the company flagship wine, Grange. Trials were run on Semillon and Chardonnay across a number of different regions, but in the end Peter Gago and team settled on a multiregional Chardonnay blend, although much of the fruit is now sourced from the Adelaide Hills. The best Yattarna to date boasts a subtle and citrus-fruit-charged core alongside aromas of smoke, cashew, minerals, and sweet spice. Tight and beautifully crafted, we'd love to have another look around 2015.

get it from...

£30.00

Berry Brothers & Rudd
Selfridges & Co.
Southcorp Wines

J.C. Boisset St-Aubin Premier Cru
sur Gamay 2005
Burgundy
France

I have written before about the
enormously talented Gregory Patriot,
the one behind the winemaking
controls at Boisset. Having served
his apprenticeship under the mighty
Lalou Bize-Leroy, Patriot is a young
man kicking goals and restless with
possibility. For not the first time in
his career, Patriot has produced a
mind-blowing St-Aubin of enormous
proportions. A tightly wound core
of grapefruit takes centre stage, while
cashew, struck match, spice, and
minerals offer up supporting roles.

get it from...

£21.49

Valvona & Crolla
Cooden Cellars
Andrew Chapman Fine Wines
Liberty Wines

Pieropan La Rocca Soave
Classico 2004
Veneto
Italy

Soave superstar Nino Pieropan
set about in an unrelenting pursuit
of quality, and in return currently
produces some of the greatest (and
most consistently high quality) white
wines produced anywhere in Italy.
These are wines that live forever.
Rich, pure, and full of flavour, this,
the single-vineyard flagship La Rocca,
is produced mainly from Garganega
grapes from the high-altitude vineyard
of the same name. Ripe tropical fruit
and spice aromas make way for
a broad citrus-fruit-rich mouthful
of wine that just seems to go on,
and on, and on.

Rustenberg John X Merriman 2004
Stellenbosch
South Africa

Hammered together using a mix of Merlot, Cabernet Sauvignon, Cabernet Franc, and Petit Verdot, winemaker Adi Badenhorst has crafted a full-throttle Bordeaux-style blend which, while looking good now, will well and truly find its groove in the next couple of years. Sweet, dark plum, cassis, smoke, leather, and spice, it's all here and bound to get better – *if* you can only keep your hands off it!

get it from...

£9.99

Waitrose
Lea and Sandeman
The Great Grog Company
Handford Wines
Seckford Wines

Weingut Bründlmayer Steinmassel
Riesling 2005
Langenlois-Kamptal
Austria

The stony terraces of the Willi
Bründlmayer estate are located in the
Langenlois, 70km (43 miles) northwest
of Vienna. This estate has a sound
ecological practice with a definite nod
to organic and Biodynamic farming.
No chemical fertilizers, herbicides,
pesticides or fungicides are used
in the vineyards, and when old vines
are removed, soil is given a minimum
of five years to regenerate prior
to replanting. This pure, citrus-fruit-
tipped, mineral-textured Riesling from
the rocky Steinmassel vineyard is
destined to get better over the next
15–20 years.

Joh. Jos. Prüm Graacher
Himmelreich Riesling Kabinett 2006
Mosel
Germany

get it from...

£10.00

Justerini & Brooks
Hailsham Cellars
Grapevine

Considered by many to be Germany's
favourite and most high-quality
producer, J.J. Prüm is pretty much
the pinnacle of global Riesling
production. With a firm grip on some
of the most sought-after vineyards
in the Mosel, Prüm is a stickler for
detail; the 33.5 acres of Riesling are
planted out on steep, unforgiving soils,
yields are heavily restricted, and the
winemaking spotless. In short, these
are world-class wines that walk the
treacherous line between acidity and
sweetness with precision and ease.
Bound to outlive you and I, don't
die wondering.

Te Mata Bullnose Syrah 2005
Hawke's Bay
New Zealand

There's plenty of buzz around Syrah in Hawke's Bay, particularly among its growers and winemakers. And rightly so – with its warm, sunny days and ancient mineral-rich, free-draining gravels, Hawke's Bay is well-equipped to produce world-class Syrah. With a spellbinding mix of sweet dark fruit, a savoury edge, a mineral quality, and sparing use of oak, Bullnose is a storming single-vineyard example that is about as complete a wine as lovers of New World Syrah could wish for.

Ridgeview Estate Cuvée Merret Bloomsbury 2004
West Sussex
England

Having endured the blazing heat of 2003, England's sparkling-wine producers more than likely breathed a sigh of relief with the onset of the much cooler 2004 growing season. Calling on all three Champagne varieties, and with Chardonnay taking the leading role, this wine shows restrained citrus/stone fruit, toast, and honey on the nose. Meanwhile, the palate is full and rich, with plenty of bright bubbles and a long, dry finish. Firm acidity and lovely fruit should see it unwind into a rich, honeyed example over the next decade.

get it from...

£17.95

Waitrose
The Wine Society
Cooden Cellars
World of Wines
Ridgeview Wine Estate

Villa Maria Reserve Riesling 2006
Marlborough
New Zealand

get it from...

£12.99

Tesco
Hatch Mansfield

While New Zealand Sauvignon Blanc continues to woo drinkers with Pied Piper-like charm, it's a handful of alternative white varietals that are really raising eyebrows across the land of the long white cloud. This is super-limey Riesling, almost Germanic in style, with plenty of citrus-fruit zip and zing. And while it's drinking beautifully now, it will definitely benefit from a stint in your cellar.

Autumn-o-rama

*First appeared in the *Herald Sun*, Melbourne/*Sunday Telegraph*, Sydney, March 2007

Series three of *Lost* has just kicked off, and I still have absolutely no idea what's going on. I give up. But to be honest, I gave up long ago after a friend rattled off his theory that the characters hadn't actually survived the crash and were in fact stuck in a state of purgatory: a kind of limbo zone between life and death. Deep, but if it puts an end to my brain strain, it'll do me nicely.

Autumn's here, and apart from season premiers galore on the box, it's also the time of year when a vineyard turns each and every shade of gold, red, orange, and brown before dropping its leaves and retiring for the winter – not quite purgatory, but somewhere between the life of summer and the dead of winter. Autumn is the season when wild mushrooms, dried-out woody herbs, greens that come with the first of the season's frosts, chestnuts, rabbit, quail, pheasant, pigeon, partridge, duck (and all those other pretty little birds my daughter likes to point out in the park) are officially ready to eat. A time of year when certain wines really come into their own.

Although there will always be the odd exception, generally you're going to get what you pay for – particularly at entry level. After all, you wouldn't buy a Fiat and expect it to drive like a Ferrari.

value

S.C. Pannell Shiraz / Grenache 2004
McLaren Vale, South Australia
Australia

get it from...

£19.95

Noel Young Wines
Wimbledon Wine Cellar
Liberty Wines

Of everything I tasted last year, two of Steve Panell's wines stormed into my end-of-year top ten. This wine could easily have been top. A combination of quality old vines, great vineyard management, and minimal intervention in the winery has produced a wine of sumo proportions. Alongside super-sexy fruit there're smoked meat, spice, and cedar smells, while the palate is rich, mineral-textured, fine, and long, with sweet, persistent fruit, great balance, and firm but slinky tannins. We've locked a few away for a rainy day in about 10 years time.

Peter Lehmann Barossa
Semillon 2005
Barossa Valley
Australia

PRODUCER OF THE YEAR

Two entries in the same book!
That's a *Juice* first. Great Semillon
produces some beautifully crafted
and insanely long-lived wines, which,
like this perennial *Juice* favourite from
Peter Lehmann, appear yellowish-
green in colour with a nose exploding
with waxy lemon, pear, and apple
character. In the mouth, it's less
angular than some we've tasted with
ripe grapefruit character and a tight
zippy finish. If you can bare to do
so, hide away a couple of bottles
and taste the real magic of this variety
with age.

get it from...

£5.49

Sainsbury's
Tesco
Asda
Oddbins
Peter Lehmann Wines UK

Stockists

A & B Vintners
www.abvintners.co.uk
01892 724977

Adnams Wines
www.adnamswines.co.uk
01502 727222

Alliance Wines
www.alliancewine.co.uk
01505 506060

Amphora Wines
www.amphora-wines.co.uk
01664 565013

Andrew Chapman Fine Wines
www.surf4wine.co.uk
01235 821539

Armit
www.armit.co.uk
020 7908 0600

Asda
www.asda-beerwinesspirits.co.uk

Australian Wines Online
www.australianwinesonline.co.uk

Averys Wine Merchants
www.averys.com
08451 283 797

Bacardi Brown-Forman
www.bacardi-martini.co.uk
02380 635 252

Bedales
www.bedalestreet.com
020 7403 8853

Bennetts Fine Wine Merchants
www.bennettsfinewines.com
01386 840392

Berkmann Wine Cellars
www.berkmann.co.uk
020 7609 4711

Berry Bros. & Rudd
www.bbr.com
0870 900 4300

Bibendum Wine
www.bibendum-wine.co.uk
020 7722 5577

Booths
www.booths-supermarkets.co.uk

Bordeaux Index
www.bordeauxindex.com
020 7253 2110

Bordeaux Wine Investments
www.bordeaux-wine-investments.com
01732 779343

The Bristol Wine Company
www.thebristolwinecompany.co.uk
0117 373 0288

Brown Brothers UK
www.brownbrothers.com.au
01628 776446

Budgens
www.budgens.co.uk
0870 050 0158

The Butlers Wine Cellar
www.butlers-winecellar.co.uk
01273 698 724

C & D Wines
www.canddwines.co.uk
020 8778 1711

Cambridge Wine Merchants
www.cambridgewine.com
01223 568991

Cellar World
www.cellarworld.co.uk
01252 703857

Charles Steevenson Wines
www.steevensonwines.co.uk
01822 616272

Codorníu UK
www.codorniu.com
01892 500250

Constellation
www.cbrands.eu.com
01483 690000

Cooden Cellars
www.coodencellars.co.uk
01323 649663

Corney & Barrow
www.corneyandbarrow.com
020 7265 2400

CostCo
www.costco.co.uk

Croque-en-Bouche
www.croque-en-bouche.co.uk
01531 636400

D Byrne & Co.
01200 423152

Deakin Fine Wines
www.deakinfinewines.co.uk
01403 248130

De Bortoli UK
www.debortoli.com.au
01725 516 467

Direct Wines
www.laithwaites.co.uk
0870 066 5689

Domaine Direct
www.domainedirect.co.uk
020 7837 1142

Enotria Winecellars
www.enotria.co.uk
020 8961 5161

EWGA
www.ewga.net
0845 450 8983

Fields, Morris & Verdin
www.fmvwines.com
020 7921 5300

The Fine Wine Company
www.thefinewinecompany.co.uk
0131 665 0088

Fine & Rare Wines
www.frw.co.uk
020 8960 1995

Fortnum & Mason
www.fortnumandmason.com
020 7734 8040

Grapevine
01768 776100

The Great Grog Company
www.greatgrog.co.uk
0131 662 4777

Great Western Wine
www.greatwesternwine.co.uk
01225 322800

Hailsham Cellars
www.hailshamcellars.com
01323 441212

Halifax Wine Company
www.halifaxwinecompany.com
01422 256333

Hallgarten
www.hallgarten.co.uk
01582 722538

Handford Wines
www.handford.net
020 7221 9614

HarperWells
www.harperwells.com
01603 411466

Harrods
www.harrods.com
020 7730 1234

Harvey Nichols
www.harveynichols.com
020 7235 5000

Hatch Mansfield
www.hatchmansfield.com
01344 871800

HBJ
www.hbjwines.co.uk
01473 232322

Hedley Wright Wine Merchants
www.hedleywright.co.uk
01279 465818

House of Fraser
www.houseoffraser.co.uk

HwCg
www.hwcg.co.uk
01279 873500

James Nicholson Wine Merchant
www.jnwine.com
028 44830091

J E Fells & Sons
www.fells.co.uk
01442 870900

Justerini & Brooks
www.justerinis.com
020 7484 6400

Lay & Wheeler
www.laywheeler.com
01473 313233

Lea and Sandeman
www.londonfinewine.co.uk
020 7244 0522

The Ledbury Wine Cellar
01531 631267

Liberty Wines
www.libertywine.co.uk
020 7720 5350

Longford Wines
www.longfordwines.co.uk
020 8676 5068

Louis Latour
www.louislatour.com
020 7409 7276

Luvians Bottleshop
www.luvians.com
01334 654 820

Magnum Fine Wines
www.magnum.co.uk
020 7839 5732

Maisons Marques et Domaines
www.mmdltd.com
020 8812 3380

Majestic Wine Warehouse
www.majestic.co.uk
0845 605 6767
(min. purchase: 12 bottles)

The Manor Cellars
www.manor-cellars.co.uk
01435 812257

Matthew Clark
www.matthewclark.co.uk
01275 891 400

Mill Hill Wines
www.millhillwines.com
020 8959 6754

Montrachet Fine Wine Merchants
www.montrachetwine.com
020 7928 1990

Moriarty Wines
www.moriartywines.co.uk
02920 705572

Morrisons
www.morrisons.co.uk
0845 611 6111

Negociants
www.negociantsuk.com
01582 462 859

New Generation Wines
www.newgenerationwines.com
020 7403 9997

Nickolls & Perks
www.nickollsandperks.co.uk
01384 394518

Noel Young Wines
www.nywines.co.uk
01223 844744

Oddbins
www.oddbins.com
0800 917 4093

Oliver Wines
www.oliverwines.co.uk
01376 571860

The Oxford Wine Company
www.oxfordwine.co.uk
01865 30 11 44

Paragon Vintners
020 7887 1800

Peter Lehmann Wines UK
www.peterlehmannwines.com
01227 731 353

Philglas & Swiggot
www.philglas-swiggot.co.uk
020 8332 6031

Quaff Fine Wine Merchant
www.quaffit.com
01273 820320

Raffles Fine Wines
www.raffles-wine.com
01453 833133

The Revelstoke Wine Co.
www.revelstoke.co.uk
0208 545 0077

Richards Walford
www.r-w.co.uk

Ridgeview Wine Estate
www.ridgeview.co.uk
0845 345 7292

Roberson Wine Merchant
www.robersonwinemerchant.co.uk
0207 371 2121

Sainsbury's
www.sainsburys.co.uk
0800 636262

Savage Selection
www.savageselection.co.uk
01451 860896

Seckford Wines
www.seckfordwines.co.uk
1394 446622

Selfridges & Co.
www.selfridges.com
08708 377 377

Sheridan Cooper's
www.sheridancoopers.co.uk
01273 298117

Siegel
www.australianwineries.co.uk
01780 755810

Soho Wine Supply
www.sohowine.co.uk
020 7636 8490

Somerfield
www.somerfield.co.uk

Southcorp Wines
www.fostersgroup.com

Stainton Wines
www.stainton-wines.co.uk
01539 731886

Stevens Garnier
www.stevensgarnier.co.uk
01865 263 300

Sunday Times Wine Club
www.sundaytimeswineclub.co.uk
0870 220 0010

Swig
www.swig.co.uk
08000 272 272

The Secret Cellar
www.thesecretcellar.co.uk
01892 537981

The Sussex Wine
Company
www.thesussexwinecompany.co.uk
01323 431143

Tanners Wine Merchants
www.tanners-wines.co.uk
01743 23 44 55

Tesco
www.tesco.com

Theatre of Wine
www.theatreofwine.com
020 8858 6363

Thresher
www.victoriawine.co.uk
01707 387 200

Valvona & Crolla
www.valvonacrolla.co.uk
0131 556 6066

Villeneuve Wines
www.villeneuvewines.com
01721 722500

Vinehaven
www.vinehaven.co.uk
01375 891984

The Vineyard Cellars
www.vineyardcellars.com
01488 681313

Vinites
www.wijnwereld.nl

Vins de Bordeaux
www.vins-bordeaux.fr

Virgin Wines
www.virginwines.com
0870 164 9593

Waitrose
www.waitrose.com
0800 188 884

Waverley TBS
www.waverley-group.co.uk
01442 293000

Wimbledon Wine Cellar
020 8540 9979

Wine Buy The Case
www.winebuythecase.com

Wine Cellar
www.winecellar.co.uk
0845 458 6116

The Wine Library
www.winelibrary.co.uk
020 7481 0415

WinePro
0772 5643 772

The Wine Society
www.thewinesociety.com
01438 740222

The Wine Treasury
www.winetreasury.com
020 7793 9999

Wines of the World
www.winesoftheworld.co.uk
020 8947 7725

WineTime
www.ewga.net
01740 821151

WoodWinters Wines
& Whiskies
www.woodwinters.com
01786 834894

World of Wine
01903 744246

Yapp Brothers
www.yapp.co.uk
01747 860423

Index

Cheers

For Carls & Indi xx

Biggest thanks of all to my partners in crime, Matt Utber and Chris Terry.

Thanks also to Jade, Chris, all the crew at The Plant and Danny at Chris Terry Photography for once again making it look sharp.

Thanks to my team: Paul Green and Dan Sims, for amazing loyalty and support on both sides of the globe; Debbie Catchpole and Verity O'Brian at Fresh Partners, for endless hard work and having to put up with me day in, day out.

To all the gang at Mitchell Beazley: Alison Goff, David Lamb, Hilary Azzam, Becca Spry, Fiona Smith, Tim Foster, Yasia Williams-Leedham, Deirdre Headon, Philippa Bell, Leanne Bryan, and Jamie Ambrose – thank you. Thanks also to Hachette Australia and Cosmos for publishing *The Juice* around the globe.

Thanks to my extended family at Fifteen: London, Cornwall, Amsterdam and Melbourne. William Sitwell at *Waitrose Food Illustrated*, Jolanda Waskito and Jane Hutchinson at *Sunday Magazine* (*Herald Sun* and *Daily Telegraph*), and thanks also to Frank Massard at Torres and Kate Sweet for helping make our Barcelona escape a reality.

To my amazing Mum (x), Drew, Caroline, Jessie, Eve, Anne, Thommo, Gin, Camilla and Felix, Team Grind; Tobe, Randy and Scotty, Gyros, BP and CC, Jamie and Jools, Jimmy and Caela, Simon and Hayley, Bobbs and Tommy, Pete and Dolly, Danny McCubbin, David Gleave, Philip Rich, Donald Stuart Gregor III and Cam Mackenzie, Andy Frost, The Joneses, Cooper-Terry, Utber and Duncan clans, Causeway Cuts (for more killer tunes), Scania and all the crew at Howies, Charles Back, Frank and John Van, The River Café team, Victoria Bitter, The Hawks, and beautiful Melbourne town. **M** x